MANAGING
FOR
QUALITY
AND
SURVIVAL

MANAGING FOR QUALITY AND SURVIVAL

A Personal Journey Toward Excellence

By

EUGENE C. BONACCI

With

HOWARD GENSLER AND RICHARD J. DENECHAUD

MANAGING FOR QUALITY AND SURVIVAL
A Personal Journey Toward Excellence

By EUGENE C. BONACCI
With HOWARD GENSLER AND RICHARD J. DENECHAUD

Copy Edited by Judith Anne Paul and Maria Paul
Illustrations by Christopher J. Sargiotto
This book is printed on 60# Weyerhaeuser
Cougar Opaque Vellum Finish.

ISBN 0-9633395-0-8

**LINVALE
PUBLISHING**
P.O. Box 119
Titusville, NJ 08560

Printed in the U.S.A.

A LETTER OF RECOMMENDATION

Gene Bonacci has captured with words many of the intuitive actions that we as business operators have attempted to use as our basic tools in our efforts toward success. He brings together all of our fundamental beliefs in such a fashion that they can be easily understood.

There is no magic to successful business management. There is no easy road to success. Bonacci's thoughts rise from the very bedrock of all successful businesses. A mission is the foundation—not some long-winded mission that elaborates all the objectives needed to accomplish the mission, but something short, crisp and to the point. Only with leadership from the top will a mission be continuously accomplished. Only if managers, starting with the Chairman or the President, understand that they must know their business down to the most finite detail will they be successful.

One of the keys in the journey to success is admitting to yourself that there are many things about your business you don't know. Once you know that you don't know something, you've got half the game won. You then go on to learn that which you don't know. Only after you know everything about what currently *is* in your business can you develop a strategy for eliminating all useless work in order to make your business function with the least amount of work at the lowest possible cost. In my view, **providing the best possible customer-centered quality product or service at the lowest possible cost** should be the mission of every company, irrespective of industry.

This book should be mandatory reading for anyone studying to enter a business career. It should be mandatory reading for any manager who wishes to operate a department, a division or a business in the best possible way. Following the blueprint that Bonacci spells out in his book requires patience, a lot of time and a lot of pain. The fruits of this discipline will be far greater than you can presently imagine.

John W. Rollins, Jr.
President and Chief Operating Officer
Rollins Truck Leasing Corp.

Chairman of the Board
Matlack Systems, Inc.

Senior Vice Chairman of the Board
Rollins Environmental Services, Inc.

This book is dedicated to my wife, Jill, and my children, Christopher, Robert and Michelle.

ACKNOWLEDGEMENTS

Gerard J. Trippitelli, my lifetime business partner, has been an integral part of the development and implementation of the Customer-Centered Quality Management (CCQM) and Total System Architecture (TSA) methodologies described in this book. We have worked together successfully, as a team, for more than 25 years. Jerry received a B.A. from Villanova University and a M.B.A. from Columbia University. He is the President and Chief Executive Officer of Matlack Systems, Inc.

Howard Gensler is the writer who worked intimately with me for many years on this book, beginning shortly after he graduated from the University of Pennsylvania. His patience was saintly, working with me writing, correcting, and rewriting the text over and over again, never becoming upset, annoyed or discouraged. His intelligence and perseverance were invaluable in developing the book. Howard is an Associate Editor at *TV Guide* magazine.

Richard J. Denechaud made an important contribution in structuring and editing the book. He worked diligently, constantly asking probing questions to clarify and enhance the reader's understanding of the subject matter. He is a former school teacher, National Accounts Manager with Datapro Research Corporation, a McGraw Hill Company, and is presently Senior Account Manager with International Data Corporation, a market research firm. He received a B.S. in Education from Worcester State College and a Master's in Education from the University of Massachusetts.

Judith Anne Paul and **Maria Paul** laboriously copy edited the text to improve its grammar and readability. Judy is a Deputy-Chief Copy Desk and Maria is a Copy Editor for *Time* magazine. Judy received a B.A. in French from Chestnut Hill College. Maria received a B.A. in English from Manhattanville College and a Master's in English from the University of Chicago.

Christopher J. Sargiotto used his ingenuity to create the illustrations from the text. He began working on the illustrations as a high school student and continued during his years as a Fine Arts major at the Rochester Institute of Technology. Chris graduated in 1992 and plans to pursue a career in medical illustrations.

TABLE OF CONTENTS

PREFACE

At the time of this writing, our country's industrial base has deteriorated to the level where it is jeopardizing our standard of living and way of life. If we do not begin to rebuild our industrial base now, world competition will make us a nonentity in the marketplace. American industry must begin this rebuilding process by putting emphasis on managing our businesses by establishing work-process-specific objectives rather than the typical departmentally specific objectives; by eliminating useless work from our work processes and making them as effective and efficient as possible; and by totally integrating all the work processes in the supplier-producer-user chain.

Accomplishing this objective requires a rethinking of our elements of managing, which will establish a system we call Customer-Centered Quality Management. CCQM provides for the implementation and execution of a new Total System Architecture (TSA), a structured methodology for executing a totally integrated universe of transactions. Although there has been an emphasis on quality for several years, this book goes beyond the typical quality objective of "meeting the customer's requirements" to a much higher level of "providing the best possible customer-centered quality products and services at the lowest possible cost."

We need help with this topic at this time because we need to change the way we are managing our businesses. If we want to become competitive again in the world marketplace, we need to start gearing our production to the demands of the world's consumers—quality at the right price. The importance of this topic is increasing as America loses more and more of its industrial market share.

I decided to write this book to lay the foundation for the necessary change that American business needs to make in order to become competitive in the world marketplace, thereby protecting our way of life. I have spent my career working in the trucking industry, which has always been extremely competitive and has had very small profit margins. You have to have effective and efficient management in order to survive. I know the CCQM methodology that I have used in management has worked effectively in allowing both companies I have worked for and their customers to provide the best possible customer-centered quality products and services at the lowest possible cost. I am confident that if American business follows the principles outlined in my book, my mission can become a reality.

This is not "just another" book on quality control with a gesture toward productivity and survival. There are dozens of good books on that subject, and few people are now motivated to buy another one with similar implications. I, however, have cast my approach in the Mission, "To provide the best possible customer-centered quality product or service at the lowest possible cost," to prove that the customer is always right, even when the customer may be out-of-line or simply wrong. Using this as a general springboard—and a focus—I show how a fully integrated program can be developed—not just with quality as a target—to assure this customer satisfaction.

The CCQM approach is unique in many ways. It is far more integrated throughout the company than the typical "quality circle" programs. It is candid, realistic and very hard-nosed. Perhaps most importantly, the details of its procedures are explicit and easily adaptable to any kind of company in any industry.

A strong point in the book is that it is a personal journey in the elements of managing and survival that the reader can associate with and emulate. Other positive aspects of the book are its simplistic, easy-to-understand presentation and writing style. The logic of the book's organization is that it uses the same CCQM structured methodology that is described in the book.

Most quality books, such as those written by renowned American quality consultant, Philip B. Crosby, advocate the supplier meeting the customer's requirements. We are advocating a totally different supplier-producer-user relationship in our book. All work processes in the supplier-producer-user chain are totally integrated, eliminating useless work from all operations.

This makes the entire universe of operations the most effective and efficient that they can possibly be, providing the best possible customer-centered quality products and services at the lowest possible cost. Elements in the supplier-producer-user chain that were once considered to be unrelated suddenly become related, using the CCQM and TSA methodologies that allow us to understand the most finite elements of all work processes and their relationships.

W. Edwards Deming, internationally renowned quality consultant, goes into great detail in his Statistical Process Control (SPC) analysis of work processes. He establishes the fact that, in any given process, there are a certain number of red beads vs. white beads (the red beads being impurities in the process), which proves statistically that the process has certain statistical parameters under which it will consistently perform and the only way to improve performance is for management to improve the process.

This book's CCQM and TSA methodologies go beyond Deming, showing you step by step by step how to improve your work processes (eliminate the red beads), which will result in the most effective productivity and efficiency. Our book addresses the root cause of American business's failure to compete—useless work—and gives a detailed methodology of identifying it and eliminating it from all work processes.

This book is designed to provide the reader with a detailed CCQM system and show him how to implement it successfully in his company, providing the most effective productivity and efficiency in all work processes. It will also allow him to accomplish the Mission, "To provide the best possible customer-centered quality product or service at the lowest possible cost." Success breeds success. Beginning with one company and then company after company, following the CCQM process will effectively change the way American business is managed, allowing us to become competitive in the world marketplace once again.

The entire CCQM system is new. The book adds to current knowledge and practice by taking a different view, teaching the reader to understand the most finite elements of all work processes and their relationships in the total universe of the system being examined and how they effect accomplishing the overall mission of the system.

The book is written for a general management readership, yet it has a level of presentation that speaks to a CEO. It is written for business, government and any other institution. I see the primary audience as CEOs, COOs and general management. A secondary audience is engineering and business-school professors and students, who can use the book as a textbook or as supplementary reading to textbooks.

The CEO, COO and general management audience will:

- understand their business, its functions and relationships in a manner that can only lead to improved decision-making;
- simplify their work processes so they require less human and system resources to operate;
- improve their company's profitability, because their expenses will be less than their competition;
- force their competition to undergo a major philosophical and organizational change if they hope to compete on quality and price;
- ensure the continued existence of their company as long as the need remains for its primary function.

The engineering and business-school professor and student audience will:

- understand the elements of CCQM and TSA, the structured methodology for developing the most effective and efficient systems, totally integrating work processes for any universe of transactions;
- understand how to solve any problem by breaking it down into its natural segments to its most finite elements, eliminating the useless elements and rebuilding the useful elements the best way possible to achieve the most effective productivity and efficiency.

The understanding of the principles outlined in the book can be applied universally by the student to his academic and professional life.

The information in the book is based on my experience growing up in a family that owned a regional less than truckload (LTL) trucking company that grew into one of the largest and best-operated trucking companies in the Northeastern United States. It also comes from my experience as Vice President-Operations of Matlack, Inc., one of the nation's largest bulk commodity motor carriers; my engineering education and training at the United States Merchant Marine Academy; and my experience as a ship's engineering officer. Twenty-five years of personal experiences as an executive in the transportation industry, working closely with some of the top industrial and manufacturing firms in the U.S. in diversified industries—including CBS Records, Levi-Strauss, The Coca-Cola Company, MMM, Monsanto, Texas Instruments, etc.—have given me an intimate knowledge of the workings of American business. This knowledge has allowed me to develop working relationships with these companies, integrating and perfecting our companies' work processes, allowing us to provide our customers with the best possible customer-centered quality products and services at the lowest possible cost. The CCQM process described in this book is the management system I have successfully used over the years, working together with these companies toward achieving perfection in our integrated operations.

The following is an outline of the contents and a chapter-by-chapter description of the book.

Outline of Contents and Chapter-by-Chapter Description

Preface

The preface talks about the book. The preface explains the need for the book and why it is being written; the purpose of the book and its anticipated contributions; the intended audiences and anticipated uses of the book; the knowledge base of the book; and an overview of the scope and organization of the book.

Introduction

The introduction outlines the overall view of what the reader can expect to learn. It states the book's mission or reason for being.

Part I. The Origins of Managing for Quality and Survival

"The Origins of Managing for Quality and Survival" explains the development of the belief system that forms the basis of CCQM. In other words, it gives the reader the insight of the author's experiences, from which the CCQM process has been developed and successfully used. CCQM is not an unproven methodology that the author is advocating as a result of his studies. CCQM is a management methodology that has been used successfully in business practices by the author for more than 25 years.

Chapter 1—"Development of a Belief System"

This chapter gives a brief biographical sketch of the author, Eugene C. Bonacci, outlining his personal, educational and business background, which formed the development of the belief system that formulated the management system that is the basis for this book.

Part II. The Problem

"The Problem" describes the root cause or loss-initiating event that is causing our country to lose its industrial base: losing sight of the customer and not providing him with the best possible customer-centered quality products and services at the lowest possible cost. It provides a powerful backdrop and overview of the way in which quality concerns have forced American businesses to rethink their competitive stance and approach to productivity, efficiency and effectiveness. This material is cast in a general way, illustrated by sound examples and universally applicable.

Chapter 2—"Losing Sight of the Customer"

This chapter explains the need for the management system described in this book. It emphasizes the importance of everything we do being customer-centered and the fact that no process in history that has not been customer-centered has survived. It illustrates the problem of how we have lost sight of the customer and how we must make satisfying the customer the focal point in everything we do, providing the best possible customer-centered quality products and services at the lowest possible cost. Finally, it introduces us to some of the fundamental principles of CCQM, i.e., being effective by finding the best way to perform a given function in everything we do by eliminating useless work.

Part III. The Process

This section outlines the 23 elements, the necessary ingredients of the CCQM process, explaining to the reader what needs to be done to correct the problem and the structured methodology—down to the most finite elements—on how to do it.

Chapter 3—"Establishing a Winning Climate"

This chapter discusses those CCQM elements necessary to create the environment required for the system being examined to survive. These CCQM elements:

1. *Needed: A Strong Leader*
2. *Learn from the Masters*
3. *Invest in Your Personnel's Development*
4. *Organize to Win*
5. *Commit to Hiring the Best*

are described in detail, using examples of the author's business experiences as illustrations.

Chapter 4—"Creating a Focus for the Entire Organization"

This chapter discusses those CCQM elements necessary to create a focus for the entire organization—to define the organization's mission or reason for being—and the basic underlying fundamental principles on how business will be conducted by the organization and its people.

These CCQM elements are described in detail, using examples in everyday life and the author's business experiences as illustrations. Those CCQM elements described in this chapter are:

6. *Establish a Mission*
7. *Develop Commitment*
8. *Do the Right Thing*

Chapter 5—"Introducing Total System Architecture"

This chapter describes the step-by-step-by-step methodology of the TSA elements of the CCQM process that specifically identify how to find the best possible way to perform a given function and integrate it with the entire system. TSA is the structured methodology for executing a totally integrated universe of transactions. This chapter concentrates on what we must do in order to be able to eliminate all the useless work from our work processes.

The CCQM elements described in this chapter that are required to accomplish this are:

9. *TSA: Decide Your Basic Transaction*
10. *TSA: Trace the Lines*
11. *TSA: Understand the Function and Relationships of Every Point of Every Segment of Every Transaction*
12. *TSA: Identify Useless Work and Eliminate It*

Chapter 6—"Systematizing and Automating Total System Architecture"

After we eliminate all the useless work from our work processes, we must put the remaining useful work elements in the best possible order and automate them in order to get the most effective productivity and efficiency.

This chapter describes the following CCQM elements:

13. *TSA: Systematize*
14. *TSA: Automate*

Chapter 7—"Managing the Total System Architecture"

This chapter deals with managing the execution of the TSA after it has been developed. You must first know what it is you are doing before you can establish who will be accountable to do it. Establishing individual accountabilities adds a human element to our schematic. Every element in the chain now has a human equivalent.

CCQM elements described in this chapter are:
15. *Establish Individual Accountabilities*
16. *Develop Performance Standards*
17. *Manage the Execution*
18. *Audit*
19. *Identify Losses*
20. *Minimize Losses After They Occur*
21. *Assign Specific Losses to Their Specific Areas of Accountability*
22. *Evaluate Performance and Measure and Communicate Loss Results*
23. *Correct System and Human Failures by Eliminating Loss-Initiating Events*

Part IV. The Implementation

This section of the book takes the reader through the implementation process of CCQM, first within his own company and then in the integration of the CCQM process with his suppliers and customers (users).

Chapter 8—"Launching Customer-Centered Quality Management"

This chapter describes the implementation of the CCQM process into a company. The author uses his own business experiences as an executive at Matlack, one of the nation's largest nationwide and international bulk commodity motor carriers, to clearly demonstrate this implementation process. Transportation is an integral part of any company's operations, so most managers are familiar with these illustrations and are easily able to relate to them.

Chapter 9—"Company-Wide Integration of CCQM"

This chapter shows the integration of intra-company departments' work processes by establishing company-wide work-process-specific objectives rather than separate departmentally specific objectives. Departmentally specific objectives disappear, and departmental structure begins to break down and be replaced by enlightened groups of employees organizing around key company-wide objectives.

Chapter 10—"Integrating Your Suppliers Into CCQM"
The author demonstrates how to integrate the work processes of your company's suppliers into your own to further refine your own work processes and those of your suppliers.

Chapter 11—"Integrating Your Customers Into CCQM"
This chapter discusses the integration of your customers to complete the loop of the total integration of suppliers', producers' and customers' (users') work processes by establishing inter-company work-process-specific objectives rather than separate company work-process-specific objectives.

The area of integration increases as suppliers, producers and users learn more and more about each other's work processes and how they relate until separate company work processes become totally integrated—a single body acting as a whole, a true partnership. Total integration will allow producer, user and supplier to work as one for the benefit of all.

Part V. The Results
In order to determine the effectiveness of the CCQM process and identify and correct its loss-initiating events, we must measure the results of our work processes. This will constantly improve the work processes toward perfection.

The "Results" evaluates the performance from using CCQM in a company and describes various concepts resulting from the use of CCQM.

Chapter 12—"Promises Made, Results Attained"
This chapter illustrates the effect of a company that has used the CCQM process by documenting the results of various company operations.

Chapter 13—"Concepts Learned"

This chapter discusses the resultant effect of using the CCQM process on various resources, activities and applications such as errors, creativity, capacity, vision, universality, expansion, perceptions and negotiations.

Part VI. Selling CCQM to Your Organization

This section provides the manager with a sample CCQM presentation he can make to his management.

Chapter 14—"Winning Internal Approval"

This chapter gives sample visual aids to be used in such a management presentation.

Part VII. In Summary

This section summarizes the author's feelings.

Chapter 15—"Final Thoughts"

Chapter 16—"Epilogue"

Appendix—Total System Architecture Methodology

"Total System Architecture Methodology" provides the reader who requires a more detailed presentation of the TSA methodology with a more in-depth analysis.

Complete integration of the supplier-producer-user chains is the way we must go if we are to survive as an economic power.

Eugene Charles Bonacci
Washington Crossing, New Jersey
August 6, 1991

INTRODUCTION

As American businesses battle shrinking markets, fiercer competition and a work force that has lost its vitality, increasing profits is no longer the issue. The key now is survival. If you're interested in reorienting your management outlook and repositioning your company for the coming years, you will have to learn to manage for quality and survival. That is what this book will teach you. It sets forth simple methods that work. Every time. Everywhere.

This book will teach you how to manage for quality while pursuing the objective of becoming the low-cost producer in your field. You will achieve our Mission which is "To provide the best possible customer-centered quality product or service at the lowest possible cost." Once implemented, you will:

- Understand your business, its functions and relationships in a manner that can only lead to improved decision-making;
- Simplify your work processes so they require less human and system resources to operate;
- Improve your company's profitability, because your expenses will be less than those of your competition;
- Force your competition to undergo a major philosophical and organizational change if they hope to compete on quality and price;
- Ensure the continued existence of your company as long as the need remains for its primary function.

PART I

THE ORIGINS OF
MANAGING FOR
QUALITY AND SURVIVAL

1

DEVELOPMENT OF A BELIEF SYSTEM

Over the next few pages I would like to tell you a little bit about myself; not because I have a tremendous ego, although it's impossible to succeed in business without a strong sense of self, but because I'm probably an unknown quantity to most of you and it's important for you to know who I am and where my ideas and training come from. Ultimately, I hope that this brief biographical sketch will help you to better understand the belief system that formulated the management system that forms the basis for this book.

✦

A great deal of the basis for the management system you are about to learn comes from my father, Marius D. Bonacci, whose teachings to me began with an explanation of the Italy of our ancestors. He explained how hard my grandfather Eugenio had worked so that he might bring the family to America, where he would not have to slave for a class of landowners. However, in America my grandfather did not instantly strike it rich. He ended up a coalminer in Pennsylvania where all his earnings went to pay the rent for the company house and buy the food from the company store. To help make ends meet, my father dropped out of school after the fourth grade and started a huckstering business with a horse and buggy. And before he was even 12 years old, he had been robbed at gunpoint three times.

From Pennsylvania my family moved to Trenton, New Jersey, where they walked three miles from the trolley station to their new home, in a mixed neighborhood because my grandfather insisted their community be diverse. Although such a move eventually broadened the family's horizons, the payback was not immediate. For many months my father would have to run back and forth to work in order to avoid being beaten up because of his Italian heritage.

My father worked very hard and was frequently exhausted. One of his first jobs in Trenton was building radiator cores for National Radiator, and later he worked with H. Carno Smith, as a hod carrier, to build the Princeton

University library. Seeing that library, even years later, made him very proud.

Eventually, my father started his own business, selling fruits and vegetables door-to-door. He was the first person to raise chickens in stacked batteries in the city, which he did in the garage behind his house, but the price of feed went up, the price of chickens went down and he was forced out of business.

His next venture was renting a gas station from a major oil company, but as he pumped more gas the oil company would raise his rent. That arrangement didn't appeal to him so he started his own trucking business —later to become the family business, AAA Trucking—by arranging with J.A. Roebling and Sons to provide them with trucking service. But he had to start very slowly. The banks would not lend him any money because he had no money.

After getting past the always difficult start-up stages of any new venture, my father started a relationship with The Coca-Cola Company that would turn out to be AAA's bread and butter for years to come. It was during this time that the two companies worked together to develop the first tank truck used to carry syrup products, a vast improvement over the previous method of loading 55-gallon drums. As a result of this change, Coca-Cola was able to automate the loading of tankers and ship syrup products more effectively and efficiently than ever before. We were constantly working with our customers to find new and better ways to improve their operations, as well as our own.

The mission of the family trucking business was to give the best possible service at the lowest possible cost. My father drilled this into my head every day. **It did not mean the best possible service at any cost.** It meant at the lowest possible cost, and all alternatives had to be examined in order to accomplish this. And best possible service meant according to the customers' standards; we adjusted our operations to their specifications. My father had an unbelievable loyalty to our customers, and he demanded the same customer loyalty from everyone in the firm.

The family business under the direction of my dad, my Uncle Sam and my Uncle Charles eventually became quite successful. Nevertheless, it was never an easy task. Constantly running into brick walls forced my father to see the need for education, and he stressed this to me over and over. He told me that a good education would allow me to do unlimited things in my life.

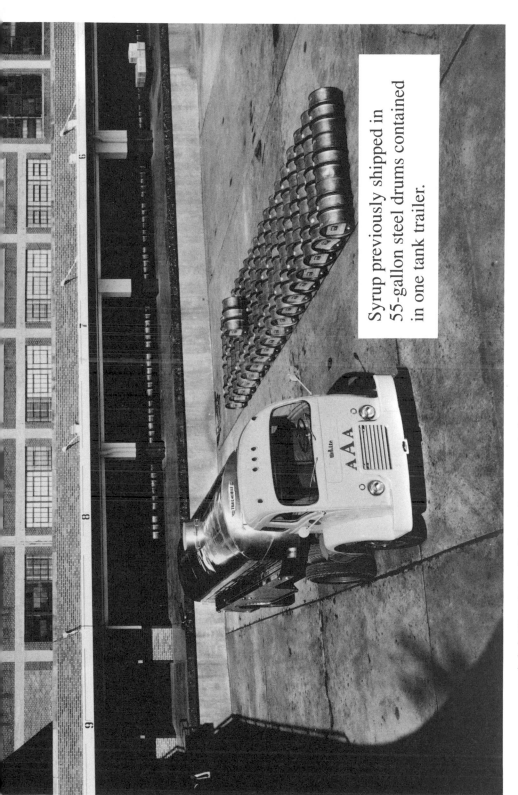

Syrup previously shipped in 55-gallon steel drums contained in one tank trailer.

AAA Trucking built and operated the first tank truck for The Coca-Cola Company.

My informal business education started when I began working for my father in the company parts room when I was only 10 years old. I continued working nights and summers throughout my teenage years until I had learned and worked every job in the business. This was in the days before computers, so I received true hands-on training regarding the entire process, which at that time was done manually.

My father took me with him everywhere he went, and he would talk to me about the businesses we passed along the way: who owned them, how they operated and whether they flourished or not. If they had gone bankrupt, we talked about whether the cause had been poor management, the owners' indulgences in things like gambling, drinking and womanizing, criminal elements taking over the company or family jealousies splitting the business apart. Often the reason for the downfall was simple: greed.

My formal education came as an engineering cadet at the United States Merchant Marine Academy in Kings Point. Our training at Kings Point was designed so that you had to work together with your section mates to accomplish your military and academic assignments and requirements, yet at the same time it was designed to make you capable of surviving alone, without help from anyone. In this education process you couldn't "screw your buddy" or take an "I got mine" attitude and survive, and at the same time you had to develop the ability to stand on your own two feet.

We were taught that there was no such thing as "I don't know." If you truly didn't know, your response was "I'll find out." And you had better find out. There was absolutely no tolerance for anyone who tried to pretend they knew when they really didn't know. You either knew it or you didn't. There was no in-between. You were trained to lead by example, which required you to know precisely what you were doing. To accomplish this, you had to work hard to the best of your ability. This training developed a resoluteness of purpose; tenacity; a commitment to finish something once you started it and the confidence to know that you could do it, alone if necessary. Your integrity and character could not be compromised in the process. Eventually every cadet developed to meet these standards or he simply wasn't there. This unique engineering education, training and experience helped me to think in a clear, logical manner. Kings Point imbedded in me further the importance of honesty and integrity in everything I did.

As a cadet and ship's engineering officer, I was required to take my flashlight out of my back pocket and physically trace each and every line in the engine room, step by step by step, in order to learn the exact location and purpose of every single valve, pump, bypass, crossover and other piece of shipboard machinery and equipment and their relationships to one another and the entire system. This had to be learned precisely in order to respond quickly, effectively and efficiently to any emergency situation that could jeopardize human lives and property. This training taught me how processes work; the methodology of executing a totally integrated universe of transactions.

After sailing as an engineering officer for a while, I worked in my family's trucking business, which had grown quite nicely over time. I learned a lot about business by working in my father's simply designed environment and also from my Uncles Sam and Charles. Uncle Sam had unwavering performance requirements and relentlessly drove us to do better. Although he rarely complimented anyone's performance, his unyielding attitude forced everyone to stay sharp. He knew if we began dwelling on our accomplishments we would lose our sharp edge of excellence, which was possible to achieve and maintain only because of the painful requirements to hone our work processes constantly toward perfection. He never let us hire additional personnel as business increased, so we were forced to find better ways to do the job. Customer demands and constant company evaluations of service and costs created an environment that promoted constant ongoing improvement whether the customer demanded it or not. Uncle Sam set high standards, but to meet them was a worthwhile challenge—and I worked as hard as I could to meet and exceed them. Uncle Charles taught me the importance of attention to detail and the necessity to sometimes let nature take its course.

Over time I have learned to incorporate and elaborate upon my family's straightforward way of doing things. To succeed, my dad and my uncles were forced to think on their own and work *with* everyone. They understood what the mission of their trucking company was, and they made sure that everyone who worked with them understood it. I took their guiding principles and the knowledge of the business they had imparted to me and wedded them to my engineering background. The outgrowth of this unique blending is a system I call Customer-Centered Quality Management.

Customer-Centered Quality Management (CCQM) is providing the best possible customer-centered quality products and services at the lowest possible cost. For me, it has been a way of life. And after 25 years in business, I can assure you that the system works.

MFQAS-2

From 1963, when I began working full time at AAA, until I left in 1979, our gross revenues increased tenfold and we became a leader in the LTL (Less than Truckload) trucking business. After a few years of consulting work with Jerry Trippitelli, my lifetime business partner—who was hired by Matlack and is now the company's president—I started at Matlack in 1982, as vice president of special services and rose to vice president of operations three years later. Implementing CCQM at Matlack has allowed the company to survive, and through a great deal of reinvestment we have positioned the company to succeed in the years to come.

At Matlack, I have taken the hands-on approach I learned from my father and my uncles to improve the company's operations. Most companies, however, do not take such a hands-on proactive approach as we have done at Matlack, and because of that they have lost touch with their operations and their customers. Their lackluster attitude to the tasks they perform and the services they provide has sent them into a tailspin. Their unwillingness to cooperate with the companies they do business with has made it even more difficult for them to reverse their fortunes.

We must once again begin managing our companies instead of allowing them to manage themselves. We must determine what our purpose is and then totally integrate our systems with those of our suppliers and users in order to achieve our mission.

This book, then, is about getting people to understand their business and business to understand its people. It's about looking at workers, the work place and the work process without the view being muddled by extraneous visions. It's about working together to put business back together one small, difficult step at a time.

PART II
THE PROBLEM

2

LOSING SIGHT OF THE CUSTOMER

DEFINING THE CUSTOMER

cus-tom-er, n. 1) one who purchases goods from another; a buyer; a patron. 2) (colloq.) a person one has to deal with; a fellow: a TOUGH customer.

The customer is always right has been repeated so many times over the years that it has become a meaningless American cliche associated with small-town shopkeepers and ''traditional'' values. It's a term used to placate angry patrons and chastise argumentative employees, but does anyone really believe that the customer is always right?

Unfortunately, no. But the customer is always right is much more than a cliche. It is the guiding principle of every successful business or organization. Any business. Any organization. For manufacturing, distribution, sales, advertising and any other aspect of a business to perform most effectively and efficiently, they must operate with the customer foremost in their minds. In the world marketplace or at the corner store, the customer rules. The customer is king. And the faster you gear your business to this fact, the faster your business can begin to achieve its full potential.

But who exactly is this customer, this moody creature with his own wants and needs that may not necessarily correspond with those of your company? Who is this person you must satisfy in order to succeed? Who is the customer who is always right?

Is it the obnoxious shopper who complains that the price of a can of tuna fish is too high, or the groom who storms out of Tiffany because he can't afford the rings, or the filmgoer who demands a refund because he doesn't like the movie? Are these customers always right?

No.

The customer who is always right is not the individual with a nickel in his pocket who throws a fit when you won't let him test-drive your Mercedes, or the individual who has a complaint about everything—service, selection, price, etc. You will never satisfy certain patrons because they are insatiable. They are unsure of what they want and/or the realities of getting what they want in the marketplace, thereby making it impossible for you to give them what they want. You're playing a losing game with this type of patron, and you can't waste your time fulfilling the fantasies of those with impossible dreams. Retaining the business of these people has nothing to do with you, so you have to assume that you're just as unlikely as anyone else to appeal to their fickle nature.

The customer who is always right is the regular, or serious, user of goods and services who understands his wants and needs and has a realistic view of the marketplace, i.e., he's not expecting something for nothing. **And the customer is not so much an individual as a critical mass, a group that will determine whether your business succeeds or fails.**

THE INTERNAL CUSTOMER

Even though we've defined the customer as a critical mass, a group that will determine whether we succeed or fail, the customer remains an abstraction to most employees of any company. The gap between employee and customer is so great that the whole process of product design, development, distribution and usage has become impersonalized. Impersonalization reduces ownership of work and, in general, lowers overall quality.

To overcome this reality, your company should adopt the view that the customer is an integral part of every work process. By making the customer an integral part of every work process, it then becomes incumbent upon the employee to satisfy fully the customer's requirements and expectations.

The customer does not have to be external to your company and the end user of your company's final product or service. The customer, in fact, can be an internal customer for each successive step in each respective work process. Fully satisfying the requirements and expectations of each successive internal customer by their total integration into the work process itself assures a final quality product or service will be achieved.

And this approach doesn't cost more money to implement. In fact it saves money because work is performed right the first time.

In summary, think of the external customer as the final link in a chain in your company. Every worker (producer) within your company must look at the next step within as an internal customer whose needs must be satisfied with the ultimate objective of satisfying the needs of the final external customer. This process integrates everyone's efforts into achieving the company's overall mission.

HOW WE LOST SIGHT OF THE CUSTOMER

There was a time when our nation's vast natural resources, innovative and expansive industry and effective system of democracy allowed us to get by with waste and poor quality and still be the world leader in everything we did or stood for. But we have become content to rest on our laurels as the rest of the world has become more competitive, providing better quality than we do in virtually everything we do. We are engaged in an industrial war that threatens our standard of living because we will not be able to continue providing income from our industrial base if we do not start gearing our production to the demands of the world's consumers—of quality at the right price. We must start looking to the root of our production problems and not look toward the government as a cure-all for our business woes. Government, even more than business, has shown a remarkable tendency to forget about the needs and wants of its consumers, and through the years it has become weighted down with pounds of paperwork created to perpetuate its own inaction.

No, legislation is not the answer. We must look to government to provide only the necessary structure and freedom to allow our mission of providing the best possible quality products and services at the lowest possible cost to be achieved. Business, through years of ineffectiveness and inefficiency, has gone to sleep on the job, and now it's time to wake up and get back to work, while there's still work left.

COMMERCIALS AND CONSULTANTS

Everything is getting more complex. Technology and technocrats are taking over. Data are piling up at an exponential rate, burying us amid the clutter. More than ever we have to sharpen our abilities in understanding what's important, for soon there will be too much to learn.

We are living in an age of media sensory overload. Commercials berate us with professional jargon and half-spoken implied truths, preying on our fears of being left behind, left alone or left in the dark. We are sold Big Macs side by side with Fat Macs (Apple Computers). Are we able to discern the difference? Are we being trained not to care?

We are living in an age of the consultant. Indispensable experts are multiplying like rabbits, their areas of expertise, it seems, not even existing until the experts themselves make such expertise available. New languages, lingoes and buzz words are turning simple issues into confusing problems and leaving the uninformed but intelligent layman—the all-important customer—out in the cold.

But has our society actually become a great jumble beyond the scope of the people, or have governments, corporations and other large bureaucracies taken common sense concepts and simply created a new vocabulary with high-priced, high-tech dictionaries needed to decipher them? In an effort to heighten our importance and artificially inflate our salaries, have we inbred a subculture of society so out of touch with mainstream customers that we have to refer to them on charts and graphs because they no longer exist as people? Are we really losing the ability to solve our own problems, or are we just losing the confidence to try?

The principles of good management, at home and in the work place, have remained the same. What's changed is our ability to realize them. Bogged down in a multitude of minute details, we've lost our perspective, lost sight of the customer.

DEFINING USELESS WORK

Useless work—which will be discussed in further detail in Chapter Five —is that work which is unnecessary in order to complete the function of a process transaction to perfection. In drawing a straight line from the supplier to the producer to the user, useless work is anything that either lengthens the line or is off to the side of the line. When useless work is eliminated, the necessary steps that constitute any transaction become simpler and easier. The transaction thus becomes less complicated and proceeds more smoothly —goods get from supplier to producer to user faster and cheaper —unencumbered by useless work.

Useless work is that which is wasted. It is energy misspent, energy that should be used for more meaningful purposes. Families, jobs and communities are all brought down by the preponderance of useless work hampering all their activity and productivity.

By eliminating useless work and systematizing the useful work segments that remain, quality is automatically improved. We simplify the work process. We are more effective. More efficient. We have more time to do what we wish to do. And we have the ability to do it better.

Unfortunately, many organizations do not recognize this and when forced to reduce costs, reduce the organization's head count without addressing the real problem—ineffective and inefficient work processes.

USELESS WORK

Eliminate it for the most effective
productivity and efficiency.

USELESS WORK AND THE BUREAUCRAT

Sociologist Max Weber said that the bureaucracy exists to support itself, that the bureaucrat hires a lesser bureaucrat to raise his or her own status and rid himself of work. The higher bureaucrat is then forced by the quantity of free time in his possession and the questioning stares of even higher bureaucrats (with plenty of their own free time) to create new work for himself—usually of the type that utilizes expensive audiovisual appliances.

And on and on it goes until there are 100 people in 20 divisions where there once were 10 people working in one cohesive unit. And to make matters worse, every one of the hundred has a secret agenda and intense paranoia, and not one has a care (or a clue) about the organization's common purpose or the common good. In its quest for greater secrecy and higher profits, the bureaucratic compound of fear and doublespeak has become a snowball speeding down a mountainside, waiting patiently for the day when its ineffectiveness and inefficiency overwhelm it and destroy *our* way of life.

In too many of today's corporations, this death-defying act is being performed on a daily basis. Meaningless new jobs create unnecessary new products-tasks-services that create other new jobs to make those products, tasks and services seem necessary. Then, either nobody buys or uses the new product and the new jobs become former jobs, or everyone buys the new hot product and it collects dust in the attic until someone creates the "Attic Organizer," which shortly after purchase starts attracting flies in the basement. Meanwhile, the staple products suffer because quality control is boring and unglamorous and supervisors would rather be taking meetings, doing lunch and designing new glamour products like "Attic Organizers." Lost is the concern for the customer, and also lost is the customer's loyalty.

We've become a society that revolves like a merry-go-round around useless work; work we do to give our jobs importance they'd otherwise lack, work we do because we don't know why, and work that has become so much a regular part of the workday that we don't even realize it's useless. Then one night at a cocktail party or happy hour someone we wish to impress asks us what we do. We answer in a minimum of three sentences sprinkled with countless polysyllabic words. And the person stares back blankly and says, "Yeah, but what do you do?"

Chances are, a great deal of what you do is useless work. Possibly you've dumped a lot of useless work on the backs of your employees.

Productivity is not what it should be, and both you and your company are suffering because of it.

The management system we will be introducing to you will teach you to identify useless work and useless workers and eliminate both from your business. Your business will become more profitable and more competitive. YOU will be able to accomplish more of your designated tasks. YOU will become more productive. YOU will become more likely to advance. Making these improvements will be very tough work. But it will not be useless.

This management system allows you to improve the effective productivity and efficiency in everything you do, providing the highest possible levels of quality in all systems in order to remain competitive.

You don't have to watch as our market shares slip away to foreign businesses. You do manage your own destiny. And if you want there to be quality in your life—in the food you eat, the products you buy, the entertainment you watch—then you must institute a quality system of management that acknowledges quality and that also acknowledges the interrelationships between supply, production and consumption.

Every supplier and producer of goods and services is also a customer of someone else's, and we are all in this together—one giant fully integrated mess that sinks and swims together. As Ben Franklin said about the founding of our Republic, "We must all hang together, or we shall all hang separately."

Needed more than ever is a management system that scoffs at "Let the Buyer Beware" and embraces a more holistic view of commerce centered around the belief—**Satisfy the Customer!**

DEFINING EFFECTIVENESS AND EFFICIENCY

Being effective is eliminating the useless work and putting the remaining useful work segments of a system into the best order possible. It is doing the useful work segments of a system the best possible way. In other words, it is doing the right things the best way possible. Being efficient is executing a system as it exists so that it is actually done as well as it can be done compared with standards for these given conditions. It is comparing actual performance to standard performance for a given set of conditions. It is doing things right as they exist.

An example of the difference between being effective and being efficient is traveling from Philadelphia to Boston via the most direct route, about 400 miles. If you could travel 50 miles per hour and complete the trip in eight hours, you would be 100% effective and 100% efficient. If you traveled from Philadelphia to Boston via Pittsburgh, it is about 1,000 miles. If you could travel 50 miles per hour and complete the trip in 20 hours, you would be 100% efficient because your actual performance was 100% of your standard performance for a given set of conditions. However, you would be only 40% effective—(8 hours divided by 20 hours)—because you didn't go from Philadelphia to Boston via the best route possible, Pittsburgh being just a bit out of the way.

The danger of useless work is that as time goes by, it becomes a greater burden that develops a life of its own. Then, on top of the useless work come useless demands that further bog down the system and create either the need for an overhaul or even more useless work. When such a breakdown occurs, the system appears to have outlived its usefulness. It is no longer effective because it no longer serves the purpose for which it was designed.

AN OUNCE OF PREVENTION I . . .

A new way to waste resources is created when stopgap measures are implemented to eliminate work that has been deemed useless, instead of redefining and refining the overall task, thus improving its effectiveness. It's much harder to plug up the dam after it breaks than to reinforce it when it's built. Like a ball team that plays hard only when it's behind, much of business puts nose to the grindstone only when things have begun falling apart. Then it is too late. History shows us that we must strive for improved effectiveness and efficiency in the work place. If we leave the door open for someone else to do better, the door will be slammed in our face by the innovator passing us to get ahead.

LOCKED OUT OF BUSINESS

For example, if a lock with 10 moving parts can be made with only 5, eliminating the useless work of the unnecessary parts, then the original design is not cost-effective or mechanically effective. Therefore, if we do not design that lock with five parts, someone else will. Our product will be obsolete.

WHAT LIES AHEAD

The chapters that follow will explain how to systematize your management structure and style around the needs of your customers and also how to improve your effectiveness and efficiency so you can serve your customers better. Useless work is sapping your productive energy, and just ahead are detailed instructions as to how you can hone your work habits and skills to get faster, more economical and better results from your business and your life.

It will not be easy.

This management system will not be a cinch to implement because it takes thought, hard work and concern for others. And removing useless work is not as simple as taking out the trash. It's part of human nature to resist change. People don't like to be questioned or threatened. Everyone likes to think he's his own best boss. Unfortunately, this is true only after we have found the best possible way to perform a given function.

You should therefore not expect immediate results when implementing the principles of the system. Think of your organization as a flabby body about to embark on a fitness program. Results do not occur overnight; aches and pains do.

To be successful in your quest to improve the production and service of your business or organization, you will have to overcome years of inertia. And you will never get all the impurities out of your system because you're dealing with human beings, and they're imperfect. But they can be effective and efficient and productive.

PART III
THE PROCESS

3

ESTABLISHING A WINNING CLIMATE

Ahead are the elements that constitute the system of Customer-Centered Quality Management. By understanding these principles, you will enact a method of managing whole processes, as opposed to separate, unrelated bits and pieces. Your result will be the continuing improvement of effectiveness and efficiency, and the attainment of a level of quality previously only dreamed about.

As you read and learn the elements, try to imagine a top-notch symphony orchestra, because the harmony that an orchestra displays is the essence of a strong leader (the conductor) totally integrating the various workers (the musicians) of the various departments (the woodwinds, the strings, the percussions) toward the achievement of a mission (the successful completion of the composition to the satisfaction of the audience—the customer).

In the classic symphonic compositions, sections of the orchestra are used in different strengths at different times to convey different moods and feelings. If the percussionist strikes the cymbals during the soft string interlude, the conglomeration of purposeful sounds intended by the artist and interpreted by the conductor to be produced by the orchestra is lost. It is the conductor's job to LEAD and UNIFY the individual talents who constitute the orchestra—all among the most individually talented musicians on their individual instruments, which are among the best made—so that they all function with a common purpose.

The conductor must be open to new ideas and interpretations, but when he decides on the path to take, his instructions must be clear and authoritative. The conductor must try to find the best musicians possible, but he can't let their individual styles overwhelm or undercut his own style or that of the piece and take away from the overall sound of the orchestra. The musician must have complete freedom to demonstrate his developed playing skills, but he must follow the music and he must follow the conductor. Freedom within structure. The conductor and the music—like the corporate

23

Have a Strong Leader

It is the conductor's job to LEAD and UNIFY
the individual musicians so that they all
function with a common purpose.

leader and the Total System Architecture (TSA—to be discussed in Chapter Five)—must maintain control.

The musical instrument itself is also an important factor in providing the best possible musical tones. The carefully aged wood in a violin or clarinet or the freedom of movement provided by a trombone slide can aid and embellish the effectiveness and efficiency of the best musicians.

When the conductor is in control and everyone is playing to his maximum ability, total integration takes effect and the most beautiful music is made. For us to make the same type of beautiful music in our own organizations, we must understand all the symphonic resources available to us; their purpose, function and relationships to one another and the whole system so that we can utilize these resources to their maximum capacity.

In business, the workers' musical instruments are the tools they have to do their jobs: a carpenter's saw, a machinist's lathe, a navigator's sextant, a secretary's typewriter or word processor or a patternmaker's shears. Are their tools the best available? Can we replace the sextant with a satellite-oriented computer-operated navigation system? Can we replace the shears with a laser-operated multiple cutting system?

The more we learn about available resources, the more we study, the more experience we gain, the more alternatives we look at, the more our universe of knowledge and understanding grows. This increases our available resources and lets us improve their utilization, allowing our universe to expand by integrating with other universes.

We become more creative because we have more alternatives from which to choose. Thus, the level of our creativity is limited only by our available resources and our ingenuity, which is limited only by our ability to learn. Therefore it is unlimited.

When you learn to trace the lines of your corporation, you will learn about Total System Architecture—the structured methodology for executing a totally integrated universe of transactions. The TSA of an organization's work process is to the products and services provided by that organization as a musical composition is to its musical performance. The TSA maintains the necessary structure to provide the best possible products and services in the work process. The musical composition provides the necessary structure to produce the most beautiful music. The TSA is the road map to reach our destination. However, before we introduce you to the process, let's first focus on your company's environment.

THE ELEMENTS OF CUSTOMER-CENTERED
QUALITY MANAGEMENT

1. NEEDED: A STRONG LEADER

A strong leader is required for the successful execution of the entire system. In addition to having complete knowledge of this system of CCQM, the system being examined and its overall mission, the leader must also be accountable for the implementation of the system. The leader must have the confidence and ability to effect change if necessary. The leader must also develop an all-star team to operate the system.

A strong leader, willing to risk failure as he strives for perfection, is essential for success.

RING OUT THE OLD, RING IN THE NEW

For businesses that start up and remain successful for a number of years, the first major dilemma often arises when a founding force decides to get out. If the old management system is deteriorating, often a breath of fresh air accompanied by a fresh perspective can be invigorating. But if the past has been profitable and the company has been built upon sound operating principles, the need to tinker can be disastrous. Too often, owners and managers set upon leaving their own stamp forget about what made the organization successful in the first place. As new people are brought in to manage old systems, one of two negative actions usually takes place:

1) new management decides to incorporate new ideas, or
2) new management decides to leave well enough alone.

In the first case, the management comes in and makes change for the sake of change, using either practices or people that worked in their previous business, or they overhaul departments so they can have their own people in place, whether or not their own people know as much as the people they're replacing.

In the second case, management takes over not knowing anything about their new business, so they don't do anything. This is not a bad strategy if you're taking over the perfect business, but that is rarely the case. And instead of using a fresh perspective to analyze the strengths and weaknesses of the new company, the new managers take the good parts of the company and don't do anything about the bad.

Rarely does new management take an overall look at what made the company what it was and work with the people who made it what it was in order to make it better.

LEADERSHIP REQUIREMENTS

To be successful in implementing this process of Customer-Centered Quality Management throughout an entire organization requires a chief executive with the ability to develop the systems and also to develop the people to operate the systems. A chief executive with such all-encompassing conceptualization skills and people skills is a rare, if not nonexistent, human being. Of course, there are many chief executives who think they have these abilities to design, implement, execute **and** resolve all resultant problems, but this is next to impossible. These different skills require opposite behavioral characteristics.

If a person is inherently creative, he usually has weaknesses in people skills, and vice versa. These weaknesses can often be overcome to a certain degree if the person is willing to understand his faults and compensate for them, but it is difficult to overcome a person's own behavioral makeup. Not every manager has every talent needed to manage.

The point is that it is highly unlikely for a chief executive to be able to put this entire process together and implement it throughout an entire organization himself. The chief executive therefore should identify the skills that he is going to contribute and then unite with another executive with complementary skills. This does not mean that there aren't other critical team members who must work together. What it does mean is that there can be no holes unplugged at the top. Find your own model and make the chemistry work and then enjoy the success of achieving your own mission.

Other lower-line management can be used to do some of the legwork, but the entire process must be completely covered as a single unit by this top management. When all bases are covered by the top management of an organization, there is no question where the organization is going or how it is going to get there. Nay-sayers are blocked off at the pass and relocated if necessary. Every step of the process is under scrutiny of the top management unit. No one can get out of line and get away with it.

2. LEARN FROM THE MASTERS

Input for this system of Customer-Centered Quality Management must be solicited from the system managers, workers, suppliers and users. You must learn from the people. Similar systems in other external applications must also be examined.

Learn From the Masters

Study models and learn about companies you admire. Take the time to speak to the veterans in your organization or similar organizations and tap into their experience. Listen—actually listen—to their suggestions and talk ideas out with them. Fresh ideas and young blood are nice and often necessary, but there is no replacement for experience. There is no substitute for years in the trenches, fighting the battles, playing the games.

Young painters often pattern themselves after past greats before developing their own styles. Athletes often appropriate the style of a favorite star before they create styles of their own. Writers often sound a lot like the authors they admire before they feel the confidence to plunge into their own ''original'' works. But in business, perhaps because of the fear of competition and the almost religious belief in corporate secrecy, we choose to muddle along, afraid to learn from our betters until they buy us out, put us out of business or die.

The best way to learn any given process is to learn from working together with and tracing the lines with the masters—those who have mastered the process you are trying to learn. You must not be afraid to seek out experience. Too often, those of us trying to learn a process refuse to learn the process from those who have come before us because we are too busy trying to make a name for ourselves by changing the process. We look at the master as being over the hill or out of touch instead of thoroughly learning the process as it exists and then building from there.

Unfortunately, there aren't many masters of an entire process readily available to us. But you can become the master of an entire work process by seeking out those who've mastered the individual segments of that process. You will have to use ingenuity and hard work to piece together this segmented knowledge, but when you become the master of your company's processes, you will be able to conduct your business with what W. Edwards Deming calls ''profound knowledge.''

Your education, knowledge and training will be yours forever. If required, you will be able to actively demonstrate the proper functioning of the processes of your company down to their most finite elements. Thus the system that develops from your studies with the masters will be based on the actual processes of the company and not some off-the-shelf solution foisted on your company by an ill-informed leader or a computer salesman in search of a sale.

3. INVEST IN YOUR PERSONNEL'S DEVELOPMENT

You must provide the management of the system with education in the elements of CCQM, the latest management techniques and leadership training. Education is important not just for those who want to get ahead but for those who don't want to fall behind. If your team knows as much as possible about your operations and the operations of your competitors, it (and you) will be at a distinct advantage in devising and implementing strategies.

You must also educate, train and motivate all of the system managers, workers, suppliers and users who integrate with your system about the system and its individual transactions—especially its mission—and how their respective transactional relationships are important and necessary to the entire system's success. Everyone who works with the system, even on the periphery, must understand the architecture of the system and why things must be done in accordance with its methodology in order for him to believe in the system and derive its full benefits. In order to most effectively communicate this information, we must have the most thorough understanding possible.

Let's talk about football. With its foundation in the modernized trench warfare known as line play, the quality of the individual players is certainly important, but their individual roles are not nearly so noticeable as their results. When the quarterback gets sacked (system failure), fans boo the quarterback, they never boo the lineman who didn't block the onrushing defensive players.

The closeness of play and the size and strength of the players obfuscate their skills. Sometimes, especially at low levels of play, the size is the skill. Whereas baseball is a sport of team-minded entrepreneurs, football is a sport of flow charts, diagrams and organizational formations. A play is nothing more than an enacted plan of action, and plans that are well devised, explained and practiced are those that succeed. A back or receiver might have opportunities to be creative in the mode of a manager in the standard corporate structure, but it is best for the team that the linemen stick to the play book and execute their jobs. Blocking assignments must be picked up, holes must be opened and patterns must be run for a play to work.

To do this, each player must trace the lines of the entire system so that he thoroughly understands how the execution of his accountabilities fits into the entire system and how the proper execution of these accountabilities is essential if the team's mission is to succeed.

Think about your role in your organization and what you are doing before you do it. Sure it sounds easy, but how many people ever think about their jobs? On the other hand, how many decide things impulsively—or with regard to personal objectives or office politics?

Which list of people is longer?

Take a few minutes a day to PONDER YOUR PURPOSE and that of your company. Start a trend.

4. ORGANIZE TO WIN

Simultaneously, while taking the wisdom of the masters, applying it to your own organization and determining your organization's all-important mission (next chapter), you must design an organizational structure that will allow you to accomplish your objectives in the most effective and efficient ways possible. In developing this structure, make sure to be open to input. Keep in mind, though, your organizational structure must facilitate the workings of the organization, so make sure that work flows in an orderly fashion. As work travels through the organization, you want to eliminate backtracking. The only direction that counts is forward. This is best accomplished by using a minimum number of layers of management. Keep the organization lean. Make sure that you allow for checks and balances within the organization so that one functional activity area cannot take advantage of another. Also make sure that people who will work together have skills and interests that will complement each other. Your accomplishments will be hindered if you do not provide for the proper implementation.

It is imperative that the organization provide for accountability of all functional activity areas, including management of the execution of the function (line management) as well as management of the function itself (staff [matrix] management). Typically in a small organization, these two separate and distinct activities can be combined and managed by one individual because he normally would have sufficient capacity for both. In large organizations, many times different individuals, one in a line position —accountable for executing the function—and the other in a staff (matrix) position, accountable for managing the functional activity area across all lines, perform the activities separately. When these activities are divided between separate line and staff managers, there is often confusion concerning their relationships to each other and accountabilities for getting the job done in a prescribed manner.

It takes a strong leader to make sure that the system works properly and that those managers accountable for a specific functional activity area (staff managers) truly have the authority to ensure execution is in accordance with design. Too many times the system breaks down because line managers execute the way they see fit rather than follow the system architecture. These line managers sometimes feel the staff managers accountable for designing the system architecture are in an ivory tower and do not understand their operating conditions. That is why it is important for managers performing a staff function to solicit input from the line organization and get complete agreement from them on the Total System Architecture before implementing the system. It is also critical for the staff manager to thoroughly understand the entire system, its relationships and execution, which, unfortunately, many times is not the case. This is necessary in order for the staff manager to take a leadership role in managing his functional activity area.

The need for staff managers can be reduced by assigning company-wide staff (matrix) accountability for specific functions to line managers with superior knowledge of that function. This reduces staff management positions and overhead, providing a more effective and efficient organizational structure. It also offers a challenge and pride of authorship to lower level managers to direct a company-wide effort and measure their results.

Just as baseball has a batting order, you too must devise a system in which the players on your team are utilized to the best of their abilities. First, you and your team must execute the fundamentals, religiously and relentlessly. Second, you must know your team's talents. Little guys tend not to hit a lot of home runs, slow guys tend not to steal a lot of bases. Some players start rallies, some players unfortunately end them, and some almost always come through in the clutch. Some players don't make a lot of highlight films or headlines, but they do all the little faceless things that make good teams great.

The smart baseball manager takes these factors into account when making out a lineup, and the smart business manager must take these factors into account when organizing his staff. Knowing where your players can best perform allows them the freedom to perform their best.

Some of the catchphrases used to describe a winning ball club are apt for describing winning businesses as well. Baseball analysts say about a hot team that ''everybody is coming together'' or ''everybody understands his role'' or ''they're playing with a lot of confidence.''

You should be able to say the same things about your team. Your players must unite as a seamless whole with a common objective—WINNING! Your players must understand where they as individuals fit into the lineup,

Organizing to Win

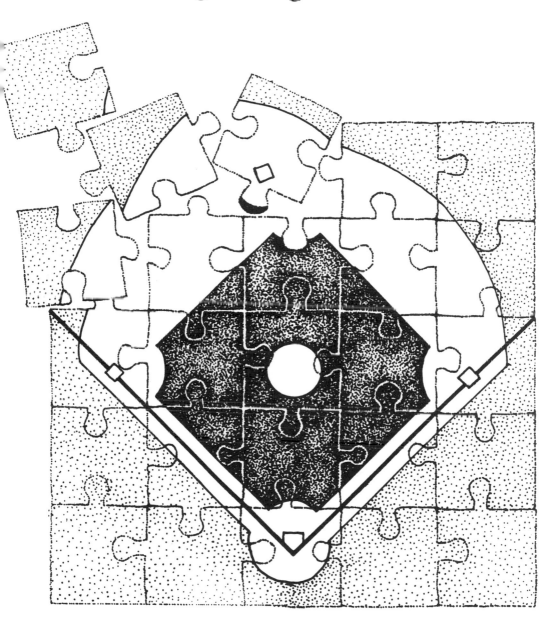

Your organizational structure must
facilitate the workings of the organization.

and they have to be given the freedom to play without fear of a bus ride to the minor leagues.

One important thing to remember, however, is that no matter how good your lineup is, if your players are not as good as the opposition's, it's going to be tough to win.

That's why the best sports teams not only have top-notch operations managers—the coaches and/or field managers who set the defenses, call the plays and train the players—they also have top strategic managers—the general-manager types who procure the talent needed to win and the financial managers who make sure the books are balanced and the cash flows in an acceptable stream.

GET REAL

At times, the manager of a ball team may wish to be the owner, or vice versa, but in setting objectives, realism is imperative. Not everyone can be king. The owner achieved his position because of the good fortune of being born wealthy or his ability to handle a variety of business activities or investments, not because of an ability to handle a pitching rotation.

Everyone has specific talents. Some people are better administrators, others are better doers. Some can oversee complex operations with large staffs, others prefer working in small groups with close personal ties. As you begin learning how to revamp your organization, it is important to begin to notice what the people around you do and don't do well. Then it's up to you to make sure they play within their limits. And play hard.

5. COMMIT TO HIRING THE BEST

Staff the organization of the system with the most competent personnel possible. Standardize your hiring procedures to help eliminate unfair subjectivity. Get input from a variety of sources regarding applicants and solicit information from past employers and past co-workers. Often reports on an individual will be glowing because an organization is eager to rid itself of the person, so try to get the hang of reading between the lines.

Don't go strictly by a resume because you're not going to be working with that usually inflated piece of paper. The interaction of workers is crucial to the success of an organization, so get a feel for the individual— how his talents mesh with your needs and his personality will mesh with your employees. Will he make the effort to learn the system or will he put himself above it? Will he be a loose cannon?

An in-depth personal interview is absolutely critical. In fact, several separate personal interviews, including other company managers, is beneficial. Sometimes things come out differently in the second and third interviews. Ask questions to determine the applicant's behavior, values, work ethic and attitudes and whether they will mesh with your organization. Go by what your gut tells you. Don't try to "wish" an applicant into being something he is not. People are creatures of habit, and you are not going to be able to remake a candidate into something he can't be, or does not want to be. Remember, bringing a new person on board has to benefit the person and his family as well as the company. If it's not a good match and a good move for everyone, you're only kidding yourself.

Since the system not only offers but requires managers and workers at all levels to make decisions, the success of the system is dependent upon the quality of the people at all positions.

Hire the most competent managers and workers to be accountable for their parts in accomplishing the overall mission of the system. Each functional activity area in the system must be properly staffed for effective execution. A weak link in the chain can cause the chain to break, and a break in the chain ends the chain. In this case, one bad apple can ruin the whole orchard.

If you're fearful of the expense of hiring the best, remember, the cost of the best personnel is often less than the cost of repairing damage caused by inferior personnel. You get what you pay for.

The best team is not only a team of stars, but a team that will work together. Put a winner together.

So far, we have tried to explain the type of climate that is needed for the necessary attitudinal changes to take place and flourish. With your corporate hierarchy in place, it's time to establish your mission.

4

CREATING A FOCUS FOR THE ENTIRE ORGANIZATION

WHERE WE WENT WRONG

IN THE BEGINNING . . .

. . . EVERYTHING WAS SIMPLE, UNENCUMBERED BY USE-LESS WORK.

In the beginning, life was simple. One-cell organisms had nothing to worry about. Or worry with. The size and mental acuity of the dinosaurs fostered a society that was slow-paced and leisurely. When early man discovered fire, prior to the invention of the synthetic log, he didn't know from fire insurance or arson or hazardous chemicals as a result of incineration. He only knew his hands were warmer and dinner was not quite so tough to chew.

Early business transactions were also simple. If man wanted fish for dinner, he went to the stream, not the frozen-food section. If he wanted a weapon, he sharpened a stick or picked up a stone. A gun store, or federal subsidy, never entered into it. A wheel was either made or received in a trade for some extra fish. Business was an eye-for-an-eye. The number of people involved in any given transaction was minimal. The user-supplier chain was two links. The person who made the decision made the transaction. A man was as good as his grunt.

IN THE PRESENT . . .

. . . THE TRANSACTION HAS BECOME MUDDLED AND COM-PLICATED BY USELESS WORK.

Today, American popular culture—especially beer commercials—still puts a premium on the value of a man's word. Even the law acknowledges the binding nature of an oral agreement or a handshake. But in reality nothing new is official until the lawyers and accountants sit down and a bank officer or two enters the scene.

In attempting to ''improve'' an already existing system, there will more than likely be a high-priced consultant from a firm of high-priced consultants. Maybe a media adviser. A personnel officer and a union head. And a slew of mid-level managers. More than likely, this meeting will also be catered.

The discussions might last days, weeks or even years and problems will pop up daily. It's a given that various factions will not agree on what path is best to follow. The larger problem lies in the fact that the various factions will not agree, or have no idea, what the desired mission is. What's all the consulting and maneuvering supposed to bring about except a bigger paycheck? There's no understanding of the big picture, no concern for the customer. Amid power struggles on the supply side, the customer-user —most essential to the supplier's success—is always the last consideration.

6. ESTABLISH A MISSION

Do you go on a long car trip without getting directions? Do you buy a Ferrari if you live in the jungle? Hop on a bus when you want to get to Europe? We hope not.

The work place is no different. Figure out where you want to go and how you want to get there. Whether your wish is to fly more people more places at lower prices or sell the best lemonade on your street corner, establish your mission.

Understand? Establish your mission!

Your mission or purpose is your overall reason for being. Your mission is also an integral part of the body of your system and must be customer- or user-centered.

Establishing your mission is critical. Your overall reason for being must be correct and exact, and how your mission relates to the universe of the total system and its individual integral transactions is most important. Everyone must have a common purpose. The mission of the company is the common fiber or thread that binds all its segments together.

One of the fundamental problems that must be overcome before establishing the mission is to understand and be able to define the total system that you are examining. This is a prerequisite because the mission must be all-encompassing. For example, if we set the mission "to provide the best possible customer-centered quality product or service" without the necessity to provide it at "the lowest possible cost," the mission would not be complete. If cost is a primary concern of your customers, then cost must be included in your mission. You can't go halfway.

Different people have different abilities to comprehend the total universe of a system; to define and understand the big picture. Most people are

Establish a Mission

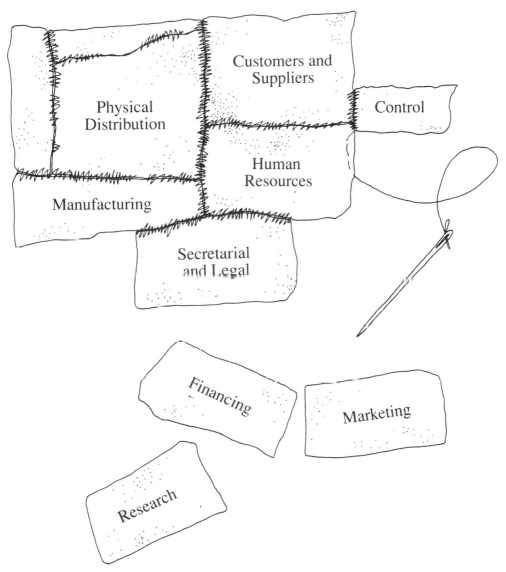

The mission of the company is the common thread
that binds all segments together.

limited by their own experiences in doing this and don't possess the time, energy or desire to rise above that which is holding them captive to their past. Moreover, the typical departmentally structured organization does not allow for the integration of all organizational operations and an analysis of their integrated requirements. In addition there is typically no leadership, accountability or authority to effect change across these organizationally imposed boundaries. These are all reasons for the necessity of a strong leader as outlined previously and for establishing integrated work-process-specific objectives, which will be explained later.

The mission, **"To provide the best possible customer-centered quality product or service at the lowest possible cost,"** is an appropriate mission for most businesses; however, missions could be such things as "to provide the most beautiful product" (painting, decoration, etc.), "to provide the most exclusive product or service" or "to provide the best possible spiritual well-being for the members of the congregation," etc.

In other words, the mission can be anything as long as it is customer- or user-centered. The mission we stated is one that is appropriate for most businesses.

This is why:

In most competitive situations, the low-cost producer will survive provided the customer product or service is the best possible. However, if your product, service or cost are not the best, the customer will seek another supplier or provide the product or service himself internally. On the other hand, there are times when cost doesn't matter. An example of this is providing one-of-a-kind items such as original oil paintings.

But situations are rare in a free market where someone doesn't begin providing the same type of product or service at a lower cost, and being the low-cost producer in that marketplace becomes a matter of survival.

When you achieve the mission more and more, better and better, every day and actually "provide the best possible customer- or user-centered quality product or service at the lowest possible cost," you will begin to *differentiate yourself from the competition*. This doesn't happen overnight. Internally, in your own company you will begin to see that the changes occurring are having a positive impact on your product or service and costs. This is observed through constant measurement of results and evaluation of performance of every step in the process. But the real barometer is when your customers begin to notice the difference in your product or service and costs and they can truly see the difference between you and your competition. When this occurs, you have truly differentiated yourself from the competition and will begin to see an increase in the market share of business that your company enjoys.

An inherent benefit derived from this process is that everyone inside your organization and those outside your organization associated with the process will begin to enjoy the benefits of system success. They begin to have more pride in what they are doing. They know they are part of a winner. They begin to understand the Customer-Centered Quality Management methodology and apply it to different applications. They begin to work more closely with their fellow workers in their own functional activity area of the company and in other functional activity areas of the company. This positively affects the interaction of all company functions to achieve the overall mission. They begin to work more closely with suppliers, increasing demands for better quality products and services from them because they recognize the quality of these products and services are affecting the quality of your company's products and services. They begin to teach their co-workers and outside suppliers the methodology of Customer-Centered Quality Management. All this has a positive synergistic effect on improving your company's products and services. And every day you continue to get better and better and better.

Why is Customer-Centered an important part of our mission statement in all transactions? The key for any process or transaction to survive is that it must be customer- or user-centered. Think about it. No process in history has survived that has not been user- or customer-centered. Any process that has had selfish objectives for the supplier, provider or user has failed in time.

The culture of the mission must be bred into an organization. It is the core of all activities. It is the driving force in all transactions. It is the basic, fundamental principle that underlies everything being done in an organization. This culture must be ingrained and become a way of life for everyone and everything in an organization. Accomplishing the mission must become an obsession.

This obsession must start at the top of an organization and eventually, as everyone buys into the system, penetrate the organization down to every single person and process.

Our mission is simple, concise and easily understood. Many times mission statements are too complicated and not everyone can make the connection between his job and the mission statement.

The fundamental underlying belief is that if you in fact provide the best possible customer-centered quality product or service at the lowest possible cost, you must check all the alternatives to find the best possible way to execute the transaction. This is necessary because you are not just providing the best possible customer-centered quality product or service at any cost, but at the lowest possible cost.

When you find the best way to do something, you simplify what you are doing. When you simplify what you are doing, you reduce the work required to execute the transaction. When you reduce the work required to execute the transaction, you lower the cost.

So, in effect, when you truly find the best way to do something, you are doing it at the lowest possible cost. You are eliminating all the costly losses in the process that require your additional resources such as money, manpower, equipment and facilities to repair. Think about any process in your work place. How many resources (manpower, money, time) are being spent on executing the process and how many more for correcting losses in the process? Most resources are probably being used in correcting losses in the process. Skill is the elimination of the useless.

Most people are victims of the confines of an organization's operational parameters they are working in. They cannot or don't have an environment conducive to allowing them to look at the process they are working in and refine it, eliminating useless or unnecessary work. Most people go to work everyday and do what has always been done, rather than being driven by an obsession to improve the organization's product or service and lower the cost for providing same every single day from now until the end of time.

This mission provides the core for the Customer-Centered Quality Management system outlined in this book to attain the most effective productivity and efficiency in any process.

THE LOST MISSION
There are many factors that have led to the proliferation of useless work but the integrity of the system begins to disappear when a company loses sight of its mission, specifically when it loses sight of the mission with regard to its customers.

An example of this is the present-day university. To fend off impending federal budget cuts and rising costs, today's large private university looks not to its age-old purpose of education for its sustenance, but to blue-chip investments, real estate holdings and supplemental services such as shopping malls, hotels and television contracts for selected sporting events. Teaching, both costly and non-revenue producing, takes a backseat to fund-raising.

The average university today employs more administrators than faculty members. A rock and a stick might have been good enough for Socrates, but a modern-day professor is almost required to use colored chalks, markers, overhead projectors or expensive audiovisual services that can repeat the same lecture for hundreds of students eager for good grades as opposed to worthwhile knowledge.

Today's professors, dismayed by the political infighting and budget battles of missionless universities that behave more like holding companies than schools, have become political animals themselves. As the role of education has diminished, faculty members have begun to take on the every-man-for-himself qualities of the business world and are so busy fighting for lenient leave policies, tuition benefits and tenure that they have little time for research or to answer students' questions.

The people who run universities — many of whom now have no previous ties to academia — are so busy lobbying for aid, recruiting students and setting up construction projects that their posts are being filled more and more frequently from the private sector's business community — often from the bottom rungs because the schools can't compete in terms of salary. This method of hiring leads to a greater turnover among administrators and further antagonism with professors, who, once tenured, may spend their entire adult lives loyal to the same institution, whereas the business types bolt at the first sign of a better offer.

In theory, universities exist for research and education. THE STUDENTS ARE THE CUSTOMERS. And the primary purpose — the mission — of the university is to provide a stimulating research-oriented environment for the interaction of teacher and student — supplier and consumer. When this function is subjugated to the financial decisions of nonacademics, when departments are cut but contractors multiply, when money is pumped into retail service industries at the expense of libraries and student services, then the society that would gain from the well-rounded education of a student suffers because the university has not done its job to the best of its ability. LOSING SIGHT OF THE MISSION HAS DESTROYED THE FUNDA-MENTAL PRINCIPLES ON WHICH THE INSTITUTION WAS BUILT.

As more of these undereducated students — or unsatisfied customers — make their way into the work force, they find themselves overwhelmed by the increasing complexities of their jobs and unable to think of ways to change their plight. They are not taught by their bosses to understand the mission of their company (or their job in it), and they have not been taught by their teachers to understand why learning the mission is important. In their quest for higher grades, their accumulation of facts was a higher priority than learning to think.

Now unable or unwilling to think for themselves, their days revolve around the completion of useless tasks, which they eventually pass off to underlings as they are promoted. But on their march to the top, their product, or service, declines because no one understands what it is they are trying to do. And the educational system and corporate system have not trained them to understand.

LOST IN SPACE

On a much larger scale, there's the National Aeronautics and Space Administration. During the years of the Kennedy presidency, when every child wanted to be an astronaut, the goal of NASA was to put a man on the moon. It was not an easily accomplished goal—worthwhile goals often aren't—but it was a measurable goal, and in 1969 NASA could proudly say "mission accomplished."

What's the space agency's goal now? Facing cutbacks on one side and a loss of public enthusiasm on the other, NASA has lost sight of its mission, and must instead use its planning resources for fund raising and survival as opposed to space exploration. Compelled to become a self-surviving profit center, NASA has been made a tool of the Pentagon, forced to market the commodity of space—and space-age weaponry—to help pay for its research and development. Where once there were heroes flying off for uncharted territories, now there are bureaucrats testifying before congressional sub-committees, explaining their mistakes and justifying their existence.

And NASA's suffering has had a widespread effect. The American people, whose tax dollars help support the system and whose national pride was boosted by the program's success, became a victim of the space program's woes. When the mission no longer existed, neither did the enthusiasm.

NASA achieved its goal of putting a man on the moon, but achieving a goal is only one instant in an eternity. The execution of a system's mission or purpose (reason for being) is timeless. The mission, by definition, lives as long as the system because it is the heartbeat of the system, not a separate entity removed and isolated from the system's essence. Although a goal is only a desire to achieve a certain result within a certain time frame, if properly executed it can be an effective and efficient *temporary* process in itself, as long as its limitations are realized.

NASA's deterioration began because it was unable to preserve the integrity of its system after its initial goal was achieved and those in charge of NASA did not work toward preserving the integrity. That is why it is better to establish a universal mission and forever work religiously toward perfecting its execution than to establish and even achieve a short-term goal that at best is only a brief taste of the greatness that can be achieved.

THE DILEMMA IN MEDICINE

Also on the government level, there's the farce of Medicaid, a noble idea which has become unmanageable because of excessive management.

In the days prior to this misguided form of socialized medicine, localized doctors provided care for their communities' poor at rates the poor could afford. The profession, highly respected, operated with a help-thy-neighbor mentality. Under this fully integrated system of neighborhood patient care, where products and/or favors were often exchanged for services, neighborhood doctors did not make as much money as they might have—they even made house calls—but they got satisfaction by providing a service they were trained to provide, and they were considered prominent, valuable members of their communities. They had a mission to accomplish.

Today, everyone has lost sight of the mission. As a result of constant bureaucratic meddling and a system that rewards impersonal health care, house calls are verboten—the poor are shipped off like cattle to be cared for in clinics. There's additional paperwork and administrative costs, not to mention additional waiting time. And with the government picking up the tab and malpractice insurance rates soaring, services that were once provided effectively and inexpensively have become ridiculously exorbitant, raising all medical costs in their wake. By turning individual medical attention into public medical attention, the paying public has been charged beyond affordability.

Originated as a means of helping people keep their medical bills down, Medicaid has brought about an opposite result owing to the enormous scope of the system and the inherent difficulty administrators have controlling it. The subsidies Medicaid has created have given an unfair advantage to medical suppliers who are allowed to take large sums from the government, which then must go deeper in debt or replace the money with cash allocated to other services. In our inter-dependent society nothing gets a free ride without something else suffering.

When a huge bureaucratic system loses direction and becomes unmanageable, it becomes easier to pull money out of its cracks, easier for the dishonest users to take advantage. In the long run, nobody benefits from such a system, and worse, nobody takes on the job to fix it.

THE STATE OF THE UNION

Unions were originally founded to provide better working conditions and higher salaries for employees treated unfairly—the union's customers were its own members. But as time has passed and memberships have grown, pension funds under the control of the unions have increased to such an extent that they have become attractive targets for corruption. When money is taken from these coffers for personal gain, the result is higher dues for members and higher contributions from employers so that the same levels of salary and benefits may be maintained, making union labor noncompetitive in the marketplace.

And if embezzlement is not the cause of trouble, power often is. Unions have become breeding grounds for would-be political candidates and power-hungry labor leaders.

Corruption and avarice cause the original mission—all missions—to be abandoned. And once the mission is abandoned, everyone loses sight of THE BIG PICTURE.

THE BIG PICTURE

How can the company (management and all its other employees) improve its work system, making it as effective and efficient as possible in order to provide the best possible customer-centered quality products and services at the lowest possible cost so that it is preserved, providing the employees with the best possible wages, benefits and working conditions and the employer with the best possible return on investment?

Without looking at the big picture in the right way, management and union leaders square off. Antagonism and resentment rule, and layoffs, work stoppages and wildcat strikes are the result. Because of selfishness, both sides—users and suppliers—are unwilling to work together and are unwilling to look at each other's wants and needs and both are faced with a loss of production and a corresponding loss of revenue. To maximize potential, all sides must work together, rid themselves of complacency and find a better way.

TAKING STOCK

A few years ago, 100 million-share days on the New York Stock Exchange were considered miraculous. Today, 150 million-share days are considered lackluster, and the exchange's new automated system has the ability to process 400 million shares a day. This new technology has paved the way for arbitrageurs and program traders, the market's latest break-through for helping the rich get richer.

Program trading allows for buy and sell orders to be put in at specific prices with automatic hedges on options and/or warrants and/or index futures. Big investors, with the aid of computers and with their bloated bankrolls to allow them to weather short-term losses, maintain greater influence and control over the market's fluctuations and have a further advantage over the small-time speculator. Many market analysts feel that programmed trading has gone so far as to alter the market's efficiency, whereas others feel that the new technology must be factored in as the new truth. Regardless, it allows more people to make and/or lose more money faster than ever before.

Arbitrageurs work both with and against (depending on whether you believe the market is inherently efficient) market forces by correcting the market's inefficiencies. Through purchases or sales at prices different from what the theoretically efficient market would bear, arbitrageurs act as short term profit raiders who play the imbalanced market until it reaches its new equilibrium.

The individual customer may not always be correct in determining how markets will perform, but CUSTOMERS, in total, always are. They have to be. What makes investing unique for the system's users is that even when they are "right," it can be very costly. The impact of the new technology on the marketplace has raised the stakes considerably, but not necessarily made the game any fairer. The system must be re-analyzed, taking the new technology into account in order to determine whether the integrity of the market's mission has been preserved.

TIME ISN'T ON YOUR SIDE

Another important cause of the deterioration of the mission is time. There just never seems to be enough of it.

Time is the one thing even the most effective and efficient manager can't do anything about, but it is essential to stay aware of its power. The passage of time erodes inspirations and, by nature, promotes change. Rapid change and listlessness are often enemies of the integrity of the process.

But time in the right environment can improve the integrity of the process as it offers an opportunity to learn more about the process and its relationships with other processes. By using this experience properly, you can then improve the process by eliminating useless work and more fully integrating it with other related processes, making it part of a greater whole.

For a venture to be successful, a great deal of effort must go into research and development. Proper planning is the proven prescription for effective productivity, so it's imperative to have every possible problem that might arise in an operation solved before start-up by breaking down the process into its most finite elements. Of course, not every circumstance can be foreseen, but every disaster can be dealt with if contingencies are made.

What often happens in organizations ranging from the mom-and-pop store to the retail franchise to the largest multinational corporation is that all the planning goes into getting the operation off the ground and none goes into keeping it airborne. No provisions are made for preserving the integrity of the system. Day-to-day malaise sets in. Catching up takes precedence over improving. And the new business takes on the properties of a rudderless glider, flying without purpose and direction.

WHEN DIVERSIFICATION = DISASTER

With the great mergers-and-acquisitions race taking place, managers are constantly bombarded with details on companies operating in entirely different industries than those with which they're familiar. A steel company executive oversees an oil business, a department store chain operates a brokerage house, a cigarette manufacturer diversifies by taking over a cookie company. In trying to dominate first their own market and then another, big corporations often lose sight of their primary mission and force themselves into positions where they are destined to fail.

Able and talented managers, hired because of skills specific to the jobs for which they were originally employed, find their talents wasted by unfamiliar tasks. To get ahead—or keep their positions at the front of the pack—they must form new areas of expertise. To stay even they must learn to process more and varied information on new duties while retaining all their old information.

WHEN MERGERS & ACQUISITIONS = SADOMASOCHISM

To illustrate this problem of mismatched mergers we'll use a pair of film companies, United Artists and 20th Century Fox.

United Artists was founded by a quartet of filmmakers who knew how to make films but not how to manage a company. After decades of classic films but poor administration, they sold the company to a pair of lawyers who were not filmmakers but had innovative ideas about how to run the company. Also, the lawyers were intelligent enough to employ the most competent people they could find to conduct the company's operations. Prosperity followed.

Almost three decades later, the lawyers sold out to an insurance conglomerate and soon went off to start their own film company, taking all their connections and most of their best employees with them. The insurance company promptly applied their successful business practices to making movies, but to their surprise, actuarial tables couldn't predict what movies people were dying to see. So the insurance company sold off the film company to a publicly traded film company whose controlling interest was held by the president of a holding company. A few years later the holding-company president sold both film companies to a cable-TV magnate who raided the library of one of the companies and sold that company's studio to another movie company. The magnate then went public with his other film company—the original United Artists—and the film company it had been sold to a few years earlier ended up under its wing, although leadership vowed to keep both companies separate.

Throughout this tumultuous period of almost half a dozen years, United Artists was sustained by a trio of series (Rocky, James Bond and the Pink Panther) dating back to the days when the lawyers ran the show. Quality films—and hits—were few and far between, and job security was bad even for the film business.

20th Century Fox was also started by film people. Fox turned out quality films for decades, but the company reached the height of success in the mid-'70s with the release of *Star Wars*. A few years later the company was bought up and taken private by a fellow who made his fortune in the oil business. He then became partners with an Australian publisher who then purchased a handful of major independent TV stations and then bought the rest of Fox from the oilman. In his first summer of ownership, the publisher saw his company release three of the biggest money losers of the season, his only hit being a sequel to a sci-fi thriller made in the late '70s under the old management.

What has happened to these companies is similar to what's happened to countless companies in many areas of business and all areas of the arts, where inspiration is usually the key factor in determining success. As more book, music and film companies fall under the auspices of more conventional businesses, and more people from the creative side leave these companies to go off on their own—witness the proliferation of new public entertainment companies—the talent pool of top management and craftsmanship and the total dollar amount available for product is diluted among more projects. By necessity, risks are minimized and only projects deemed safe are undertaken.

A proper mix of talents is needed to run any company, but especially in arts-related companies where the creative process is a key element in achieving success. Artists who have a commercial sensibility know and manage the creative process in their brain intuitively—something incomprehensible to by-the-book businessmen—and many executives at film studios or book publishers have not been astute enough to identify, capture and manage this process transaction. They're both unwilling and afraid to give control to the very people upon whose talents their success depends. On the other hand, the artists and craftsmen have tended not to be particularly adept at managing multimillion-dollar companies, where intuition alone doesn't pay the bills. That is why a balance must be struck, with everyone understanding the mission of the company and working *together* on this mission.

By putting the bottom line above all others—remember it's the bottom line, not the top line—and taking the power to determine ''go'' projects away from the creative people weaned on the industry and its creations, all the creative fields begin to suffer. Creative people get into creative fields because these fields are businesses in concert with their own behavior and values. It is only logical, in any endeavor, that if your belief system is in harmony with your tasks and objectives, then you will have a decision-making system that is better attuned to positive results.

To the moguls who founded the TV, movie, radio, book or Broadway industries, the mission was to make the best product at the best cost available to the most people at the best price. To today's executives, it's all business, and the goal is to make the biggest profit, leaving out the most critical part of the system, the creative process. That goal may be considered appropriate to some, but it is a short-term goal that discounts the notions of tradition and loyalty as keys to long-term success.

The founders of the creative industries understood that getting to the audience was only half the battle. The consuming public also had to be entertained. Then they would come back again and again. It was customer loyalty that created the big movie stars, not demographics research and ancillary rights. Give me a good picture and I'll come back to see your next one. But stiff me with a turkey and I'll stay home and watch television or the VCR, or read a book. With so much competition for the leisure dollar, this is not the time for entertainment companies to scrimp on entertainment. In the arts, like everything else, THE CUSTOMER IS ALWAYS RIGHT. And when the customer is not satisfied, he looks elsewhere.

THREE QUICK POINTS

The best writer, best actor and best director don't add up to the biggest hit if the inspiration is absent. In any industry, full commitment to a project and total belief in its ability to succeed are essential if the project is to be viable. More money isn't always the answer; nor is more paperwork. What makes a work of art is what makes an athletic superstar, or a top politician, or a first-rate business:

1. Understand your mission: Know where you want to go and why you want to go there.
2. Focus: Once you understand your mission and its importance, concentrate on how to achieve your objectives and how to sustain them.
3. Have Integrity: Once you are on the road to success, don't waver, don't look for the easy way out, and don't give up.

7. DEVELOP COMMITMENT

Once your mission is established, BECOME A MISSIONARY. Preach the gospel. Build enthusiasm. Commitment must start with the top management of your organization and become a way of life. You are like the rabbit at the dog track. If you don't run, the dogs won't run. You have to set the pace for the greyhounds.

But YOU can't do it alone, and there's one factor that will help you win converts: people like to be part of a winner.

Instill in your associates the same sense of pride and purpose you've

Three Quick Points

UNDERSTAND YOUR MISSION: KNOW WHERE YOU WANT TO GO
AND WHY YOU WANT TO GO THERE.

FOCUS: ONCE YOU UNDERSTAND YOUR MISSION AND ITS
IMPORTANCE, CONCENTRATE ON HOW TO ACHIEVE YOUR
OBJECTIVES AND HOW TO SUSTAIN THEM.

HAVE INTEGRITY: ONCE YOU ARE ON THE ROAD TO SUCCESS,
DON'T WAVER, DON'T LOOK FOR THE EASY WAY OUT,
AND DON'T GIVE UP.

instilled in yourself. They'll work harder AND enjoy themselves more. Should they rebel and refuse to become players on your high-flying, hustling team? Relocate them. You can't allow a few sour apples to destroy your system, which is providing benefits for everyone.

One important way to develop commitment is to solicit input from all system management, workers, suppliers and users.

In addition to examining systems in both competing and unrelated businesses, input should be gathered from those who work above, under and with you. Providing input allows someone to feel his role and opinion matter, thereby stimulating productivity. Allowing for input also provides a surprising number of helpful suggestions for maximizing effective productivity and efficiency.

But remember, suggestions aren't automatically good. It is up to the leader to synthesize the input and eliminate the useless before implementing change.

But teams that play hard are not only those that feel they have a stake in their operations and their outcome, but also those that feel the game or race is never over. Since the game of business has no time limitations and therefore never ends, it is important to stress that the march to a perfect work environment also never ends. Searching for the most effective and efficient way of performing one's work is a never-ending mission.

You can convey this message in a number of different ways:

Support from the Top—Every important link in the chain, from the president to the maintenance workers, is behind the system of Customer-Centered Quality Management. As we see far too frequently in government and in many organizations, when individuals work at cross purposes or without clear direction, problems arise. It might be something as minor as two salespeople calling on the same client or as major as the Iran-Contra mess.

Leadership from the top not only works to inspire the troops, but it also makes it easier for everyone else's role to fall into place. Leadership from the top also sends a clear message to customers, associates and competitors about what it is you and your organization stand for. And when the senior managers understand the tasks and problems facing their workers, it makes for a more constructive relationship between employer and employee and a more productive work place.

Stability in Management—Like that old ode to loyalty "You should dance with the one that brung ya," such is the case of well-run companies where a trusting give-and-take relationship exists between management and the work force. Workers must feel that good performance will lead to higher pay and/or promotions or some other fringe benefit to be negotiated, and managers must feel their service to an organization will not leave them subject to the hiring and firing whims of a revolving-door corps of executives.

Make an effort to reward your people for a job well done and make them feel they are an important part of the company as a whole. Do your best to promote from within, not just because you want your employees to strive for a higher position and more accountability, but because they will be most familiar with what it is they are supposed to accomplish and best suited to achieve your objectives.

Strive too for a stable management group, so that insiders and outsiders can deal with familiar faces and receive consistent messages. It's difficult to find successful organizations that have constant turnover at any level of their operation, because it's difficult to plan for the future when the future is not definite.

Stability is the key. Find good people, allow their jobs to be as stimulating as possible, and then do everything you can to keep them.

The Star System—Just as movie studios recognize their stars, recognize yours, because they are the De Niros, Streeps and Nicholsons of your company. They're the people whose work and dedication sets you apart from your competition. Therefore, they must be made to feel important. When you see success in implementing the CCQM process or the achievement of outstanding results, management should recognize the principals and encourage them to showcase their success at management meetings. This showcasing of achievement not only allows the workers a direct line to management and direct feedback from their bosses, it also forces management to interact with its workers and instills respect on both sides.

Peer Tutoring—Since managers don't have the time to give private help to all workers who are not up to standard, and manager-worker sessions often lead to performance insecurity and adversarial relationships, try pairing up your finest managers with those who require additional time and help. It is important, however, to stress that learning from a co-worker is in no way embarrassing or a cause for concern. The cause for concern comes from not learning.

Training, Training, Training—Provide job and system training to EVERY employee in the company. Even train the trainers. There are no exceptions. By making everyone undergo training, you demonstrate your allegiance to CCQM by word and deed. If everybody's got to do it, it must be important.

Mastery Learning—When managers and workers don't master CCQM and/or their specific job tasks, they are required to go back to the beginning of the process and redo it until assigned tasks are done properly. You don't want your teachers to be shaky on their lesson plans. There are two ways to perform organizational tasks: correctly or incorrectly. Only one way is acceptable.

Design a structured environment in which certain jobs are to be performed certain ways. Until those performing those jobs convince you that they have found better ways—and it is important always to remain open to that possibility—they are instructed and obligated to do things the way you want them done. If you set standards but don't force people to live up to them, then you have not set standards. To succeed, YOU must have standards.

BE POSITIVE

A positive view of people is important because it inspires reciprocity. You want people to have a positive view of management, both inside and outside your company, and this objective is embodied by your training mission.

When you train your employees, set out to:
-develop an internal source of qualified candidates;
-impart to them the practical knowledge and skills required to perform their jobs;
-have them internalize their mission and become fully versed and committed to the CCQM process.

◆

THE PRELIMINARIES

With a driven, dedicated and skilled work force in place, it is essential to set up an environment that accentuates the positive. Instead of ripping apart your present structure and staff, look at what you have as a base—a beginning. If you spend all your time ferreting out guilty parties—any mistakes being made are probably ones that have been made for years—you'll never get anywhere. There's no reason to get bent out of shape now that you're on the verge of major improvements to your organization.

Stay Upbeat—You're asking people to change the way they think and act, and the way they think of themselves in relation to your company. Whereas they previously may have been reporting to a job, now you're asking them to be a part of something. Many employees will welcome the change. Some will be suspicious. Some were happy in the anonymous cocoon where they functioned for years. You will have to be part manager and part psychiatrist, looking for the right buttons to push to get your different personalities in line.

Establish a Quality-Engineering Department—Individuals in this department will oversee the implementation of Customer-Centered Quality Management throughout your organization. Their presence and their performance will ensure CCQM's implementation without drawing time away from managers, who will be able to continue focusing on executing the work processes to perfection.

The quality-engineering department will be the equivalent of a consulting firm brought in to improve your operations. Their charge will be to examine your operations with objectivity. They should divorce themselves from office politics and the "old way" of doing things. What makes this "consulting firm" such an asset, however, is that it is not an outside group. These are your people. If they understand and have been trained correctly and are sufficiently motivated, then they have the long-term interests of the company at heart. However, it may be necessary to bring in an outside consulting firm to work with you. Don't be afraid to do it if you need the help.

At company meetings, the quality-engineering group also has the clout to spur discussion about areas where CCQM implementation and bottom-line profitability SEEM to be at cross purposes. Through a company-wide examination of such problem areas, new methods of doing things and new ways of looking at them are often found. Remember, your mission is to better serve your customers, and achieving this mission will result in stability and long-term profitability. Don't get sidetracked.

Communicate Results—As CCQM is being implemented, have everyone sign off on the operation strategy, then track and broadcast all your little victories. You want everyone to share in the joys of your success. Demonstrate the relationship between CCQM and sales and earnings results. Keep the message in front of everyone through constant repetition in various media—posters, personal letters, slide presentations, etc. Your workers have to believe their sweat is making a difference, and they will perform better if they know how their peers are doing. Nobody likes to be at the bottom of the pack. Good communication is not only necessary, it's essential.

Reward Success—Share the fruits of victory with all and let the achievers know you're truly proud of what they're doing. Although it is not unreasonable to expect workers to perform the tasks they were hired to perform competently, human beings require feedback. Let your people know that what they're doing isn't easy and that you appreciate their efforts. A job well done deserves positive feedback—through commendations, promotions and/or bonuses. True, success is frequently its own reward, but success alone doesn't pay the mortgage. Also, it's often a good idea to reward outstanding achievers with plaques and awards at your monthly and/or annual meetings. That way, no top performer goes unrecognized.

8. DO THE RIGHT THING

Always do what is right and in the best interest of the system. This not only enforces the character of the system but also develops the character of the people working within it. Don't be lured by quick fixes or quick bucks. Work within the confines of the system that you've worked so hard to create. You're an orchestra musician, a utility infielder, a supporting actor working for the whole and not for yourself.

Before taking actions that will affect the system, imagine their effect. If you think in terms of the entire system as opposed to your specific part of it, you will be well on your way toward doing the right thing. And when you do the right thing, the preservation of the system becomes academic.

It is easy to make popular decisions that offer people a false sense of happiness. It is easy to make selfish decisions that give you a false sense of accomplishment. These decisions, however, will not be in the best interests of the system. But if you make your decisions with regard to the big picture, they will ultimately be in everyone's best interest and work to develop both the character of the system and its people.

Often, by making an unpopular decision, you will be held in contempt and not be given credit for preserving the purity of the system. Don't worry. This isn't "Death of a Salesman," and popularity isn't everything. Eventually the improved effectiveness and efficiency of your organization will prove you right, and your associates will stop hanging you in effigy.

Remember, even the best decisions breed a certain amount of resentment. But also remember that just because a decision is unpopular doesn't mean that it's correct.

"Always do what is right and in the best interest of the system" may appear to be a dangerous statement; but, if in fact the architecture of the system is correct you must always do what is best for the *entire* system because it is the system that is providing for all its individual parts. It is the system that is providing for its users, producers and suppliers.

Character is the degree that something or someone will go to to do what is right. Everything and everyone has varying degrees of character. If we do what is right and in the best interest of the system, we develop the character of the system and its people. When we do this, the preservation of deriving the best possible benefits from the system for everyone and everything associated with it becomes academic. Also, this is a necessary requirement to preserve the continuity of the system itself.

When implementing a system, people naturally resist change and therefore attempt to retain certain segments of the original system. In other words, they try to keep doing things the way they have been done in the past. It is easy for the leader to compromise the system in order to avoid conflict and keep the people happy. However, the integrity of the system cannot be violated. If necessary, large systems with multiple integrated segments should be implemented in stages rather than by compromising any segment of the system. This allows the system to be more easily learned and digested by the people operating the system. It is also possible for certain people in the system to try to sabotage the success of the system by deliberately performing their job functions in a manner to not get successful results. This is done in an effort to wear the leadership down and not allow the system to obtain favorable results. The operation of the system then becomes bogged down and ineffective. This is a typical bureaucratic passive resistance to change where the people operating the system work on the premise that the current leadership advocating the change will eventually be replaced by new leadership with different ideas. The people operating the system basically are more entrenched and persevering and outlast the leadership. That is why a strong leader is necessary who will not allow this to happen; one who can show the people himself, if necessary, how to operate the system.

This is also the reason why the methodology of the Total System Architecture and physical operation of all segments of the system must be thoroughly tested to ensure they will most effectively and efficiently work before implementation. Nothing worse can happen than for a system to get bogged down because it was designed or set up to be operated improperly with the end result that the system fails. Your credibility is on the line. Don't let it be destroyed. You can't let the system operators prove to you the system won't work. You have to prove to them that it will work. And believe me, it is a challenge that is going to require your total resources to effect this change. That is why you can do only so many changes at one time. Don't take on more than you can get done successfully. Don't bite off more than you can chew at any one time. This process is going to take time, and it is never going to end. You can't do it overnight. You are changing the culture of your organization. You must and can prevail.

MANAGE THE RIGHT THING

If you are reading this book, you probably have some familiarity with the elements of management.

1) *Establish Objectives*

2) *Direct the Attainment of Objectives*

3) *Measure Results* are more than likely a few of the basic management principles you've been taught.

The essential problems with these teachings, however, is that we are not being taught to manage the right thing. We should be managing the entire process transaction (the big picture) instead of just concentrating on the various functions in the process (the small dots).

Too many times we become so absorbed in managing a specific element of a transaction that that element becomes the driving force of the transaction. We lose sight of that element's relationship to the whole process —managing it as a universe unto itself—and how it needs to be managed in order to complement the whole process and make the whole process as effective and efficient as possible. This prevents us from doing what is right and in the best interest of the system.

Many times statistical limits are used to measure the performance of a specific element in a process, which causes managers to become so involved with meeting numerical parameters that management lose sight of what the entire process is trying to accomplish. Measurement of results by statistical process control is important and must be an integral part of the total process methodology, but it must be done in such a way that it complements the achievement of the mission of the total process.

In the competitive world of business, managing the right thing is a prerequisite to WINNING: doing what you do better—more effectively, more efficiently and with a lower cost—than anyone else. And winning will become possible only if you understand the big picture when you set out on your mission.

◆

So far the CCQM process has forced you to examine your work place, your work force and your objectives. Now it is time to get down to the nuts and bolts of developing the Total System Architecture (TSA).

5

INTRODUCING TOTAL SYSTEM ARCHITECTURE

There's an old joke about a man who goes to a doctor's office. With the doctor peering at him, the man raises his arm above his head.

"Doctor," he says, "it hurts every time I do that."

"So don't do that," the doctor advises.

Eliminating useless work in your completely integrated CCQM work processes isn't quite that simple. But as the necessary steps for improving effectiveness and efficiency are outlined in the pages that follow, you will see that it's almost that simple. You just have to understand what not to do.

Useless work items are not going to be things like "don't make multiple copies of lengthy reports when only one person in your office can read," or "don't put the coffee machine on the side of the office where people drink milk" or "prohibit workers with sick children from using their telephone for personal calls." Useless work is far more insidious, because it stems more from the system than the workers.

The system is what allows workers to revel in laziness, and it is that same system that forbids punishment for poor work. Given a chance, and an environment in which it is possible to thrive, most workers will jump at the opportunity. Those who don't are not suited for their present roles and should be transferred to a job that makes better use of their talents.

◆

When a first-year biology student dissects a frog, he doesn't slap the thing down on a table and take out an axe. He looks at it, sniffs it, picks at it, prods it and finally cuts away at it with mincing movements designed to shear away the unnecessary layers and get better access to the individual organs.

In order to improve the way your organization functions, you must first dissect it and look at each of its component parts separately. Then, like a surgeon, you must piece it back together with reinforcements. Through poor management, the lifeblood of your company—and in many ways your life —is being sucked away. By taking your organization apart and putting it back together you are performing a transfusion, giving an extra boost to a bloodstream that will flow more freely without the clotting currently taking place.

The body functions as a unit, with the organs functioning separately but dependent upon each other for sustenance. The brain cannot process data without the heart pumping blood, and the heart won't pump without signals from the brain. During surgery, all relevant body parts must be cared for when one is in need of repair. Machines that do the work of various organs have enabled doctors to search for more long-term methods to mend them. But the machines currently work only as stopgap measures. For proper health, the body must function on its own.

For proper organizational health, the entire unit must also function as one. Each individual organ may, and must, perform on its own, but the understanding must always be there that the organ, or office, is not alone. In every organization, and every transaction performed by every part of every organization, the different segments are interdependent. For maximum effectiveness and efficiency, each tiny part must perform at its best if the sum is to be all it can be.

But the elimination of useless work is not accomplished via the aid of a quick fix or an old adage. Rare is the situation that is so ineffective or inefficient that it must be destroyed in order to be made useful. Normally, tinkering and tightening work if the approach starts at the roots. The key point to keep in mind is to catch problems early. Once the flood starts, a plumber with a flashlight is of little value.

Useless work is equivalent to the buildup of plaque on your teeth. Sometimes simple brushing on a daily basis will do the trick. Other times, a thorough cleaning by a dentist is required. On rare occasions more serious work is needed.

For most people plaque could be avoided by doing a number of simple things stressed by parents everywhere. Cutting out sweets, flossing and regular brushing will go a long way to avoiding big medical bills in the future, but who thinks of long-term benefits when tempted with a piece of chocolate cake? So it is in the work place, where little bad habits build up until major surgery is needed to repair the damage.

Most people know that what they're doing is not in the best interests of a sound and healthy business, but inertia has set in to the point where caring seems both useless and unpopular. Still, there are many workers, especially those new to the system, who are unaware that things could be done better, faster and cheaper.

But these are exactly the people whose attitudes must be changed. The rising executive, the new department head and the novice secretary, just like the hot athletic prospect, are the ones with the power to make a difference during their ascendancy. To do so, they must be given the freedom to think and make mistakes without fear of removal. They must be allowed to evaluate their personnel and their daily tasks without worry that their priorities will differ from someone else's.

It is the role of each successive superior to mesh the various priorities into a cohesive whole with a unified purpose, and it is also his role to work with his employees so that no one feels left out in the cold.

Much of this is common sense, but as you look around you throughout your daily activities, how much common sense do you see?

◆

In order to facilitate your enacting the ideas discussed so far, here begins a checklist of the Total System Architecture methodology. This entire process of breaking down the system into its most finite elements and rebuilding it must be documented with flow charts and narrative. Remember, this includes the total integration of all automated (MIS) and physical field operations, including the step-by-step-by-step methodology of the thinking process of the human beings into the system that determines how they naturally perform their functions. The way the human being naturally performs a work process mentally and physically must be made an integral part of the system if the system is to be truly understood and is to be ultimately restructured to function as effectively and efficiently as possible.

9. TSA: DECIDE YOUR BASIC TRANSACTION

To identify your basic transaction, ask yourself what is the individual whole transaction within your organization's work process that describes your product or service. **Of all the tasks you and/or your company perform in a day, what is the fundamental transaction that drives your business—the one thing that you must do or your organization would have no reason to exist?** This is your basic transaction and this is the transaction that must be foremost in your management scheme.

It is critical that you understand your company's basic transaction because you must be able to define it and its importance to the process so that you can understand how and why it drives your business and also be

The Fundamental Principles of
Total System Architecture

OBSERVE AND UNDERSTAND THE UNIVERSE OF THE SYSTEM
YOU ARE ANALYZING AND KNOW ITS MISSION.

DIVIDE THE UNIVERSE INTO ITS MOST LOGICAL,NATURAL,
SMALLER PORTIONS, WHICH IN THEMSELVES REPRESENT
WHOLE TRANSACTIONS.

ANALYZE EACH SEGMENT OF EACH TRANSACTION UNTIL IT
IS FUNCTIONING IN ITS SIMPLEST FORM IN COMPLETE
FREEDOM FROM ANY ENCUMBRANCES OF USELESS WORK.

REBUILD THE UNIVERSE SYSTEMATICALLY ONE STEP AT A
TIME, STEP BY STEP BY STEP, WITH THE PURE, USEFUL
WORK SEGMENTS OF EACH TRANSACTION.

NEVER ALLOW ANY IMPURITIES OF USELESS WORK TO
ENTER OR RE-ENTER THE UNIVERSE.

able to explain its significance to others in your organization.

It is essential that you understand the methodology of the basic transaction because if your company is to strive for perfection, it must strive for perfection in performing its most fundamental task.

Key to perfect execution of the basic transaction is universal agreement among all personnel as to what the basic transaction is. Deciding the basic transaction, therefore, can not be left solely to upper management. Managers at the top must review their decision with field personnel in order to refine it and get company-wide approval. Without everyone on the same page, success is impossible.

Deciding the basic transaction could take minutes if your company is already focused and well managed, but it should take no more than a couple days to conceive it, refine it and reach total agreement upon it. And during that time, your company should be operating under business-as-usual conditions. By staying within the field of battle and not trekking off to Aruba for an upper-management powwow, you will demonstrate the importance of the decision you are about to make and be better able to make it because you will be able to factor in all of your organization's daily transactions as they occur.

Keep in mind that the basic transaction is like a high-concept movie plot: if you can't say it in a sentence, it's not basic enough. In fact, the nature of this transaction is often so obvious that managers refuse to believe that simply stating it can positively affect the way they do business. Don't be afraid of the obvious.

Having decided upon the basic transaction, it must then be broken down into its most finite elements for it must form the foundation of the Total System Architecture to generate from or allocate to all costs, profits and other measurements of performance. The basic transaction is the service- or product-creating event within your company. It generates the costs that are directly associated with providing your product or service, and all peripheral costs can be allocated to this basic transaction. Profit and other performance centers are generated and allocated in the same manner.

In order to most effectively and efficiently control and analyze these areas, your measurements of performance must be transaction- or process-specific rather than departmentally specific.

Typically, these performance centers are measured and controlled on a departmental basis, and departmentally specific performance factors are prorated over many process transactions. This type of measurement does not provide for the detailed process analysis necessary to manage the execution and constantly improve the process. Using the transaction- or process-specific allocation methodology, the only performance measurements that are prorated are those that are impossible to allocate to a specific transaction or a process, which should be minimal if your basic fundamental transaction is properly defined.

You can build all profit centers, cost centers and other performance centers from this basic fundamental transaction. You are able to do this because all measurements can be broken down—or built up—however you choose, maintaining their integrity with the specific transactions.

What you are doing is charging each specific transaction for the actual costs it incurred and measuring its other actual performance factors. By allocating the costs and other performance factors to each specific transaction, you can then identify areas of lower or higher cost or better or poorer performance in specific areas of specific transactions that will allow you to improve the process. Profitability and other performance studies for specific transactions or groups of transactions also become possible. Pricing decisions can be better made, fully understanding actual costs. By breaking down the transaction into its most finite elements, you can also look at common elements of multiple transactions for the same purposes. Allocating costs and measuring performance departmentally does not allow you to make this kind of analysis. Your accounts payable and general ledger systems must be structured to provide for this transaction specific allocation methodology.

All other system transactions are driven by the basic transaction. System transactions are the peripheral transactions in the universe of transactions, both internally within your organization and externally to your organization, which are required to support or are somehow affected by their relationship with the basic transaction.

You have to step back, take a deep breath and take a fresh look at your business.

10. TSA: TRACE THE LINES

Except for defining a mission and deciding upon your basic transaction, everything else in the Total System Architecture we've begun to outline is generic. Good management is a constant—transferrable to any organization. Corporate objectives may change and individual accountabilities may change, but a solid foundation for enacting change will stay solid. The fundamental principles and methodologies described here have universal applications and, if implemented, will make your organization function most effectively and efficiently, providing for its preservation.

Whole transactions are the individual complete transactions that make up a work process.

Each work process consists of a single whole transaction or multiple whole transactions.

A fundamental transaction is the primary transaction of a group of multiple transactions that make up a work process.

The basic transaction is the fundamental transaction of the primary work process.

So, how do you trace the lines?

1. The entire universe of the organization's total system should be broken down into its most logical, natural, smaller work processes.
2. Then, each respective work process within the total system should be broken down into its natural whole transactions.
3. Then, each whole transaction within each work process should be broken down into its natural segments.
4. Then, each segment of each whole transaction should be broken down into its most finite elements.

Each respective work process within the total system should be traced one work process at a time, step by step by step.

Everyone will understand the business and what makes it tick. The key to this understanding is your flow-charting. Once you take your flashlight out of your back pocket and trace the lines, step by step by step, you must develop written procedures for all operations. Even though you are looking to improve your existing system, it is necessary to flow-chart it in order to understand completely all the total system requirements that are necessary and are presently being provided for so that you ensure they are provided for in the new system design. If you don't do this, many of the things you're already doing right will be overlooked or mistakenly eliminated. The new system will then be inadequate for the system's requirements. Then you're back where you started from with two important differences: you've wasted time and money for your first reorganization, and your work force has lost faith in your abilities to turn things around.

The root cause of many new system failures is often the failure to consider something as obvious as the system's requirements. System managers are then forced to return to the old system or modify the new system rendering it less effective. It is critical that the new Total System Architecture work as designed when it is implemented.

Flow-charting like this should be performed by quality engineers, MIS system engineers and analysts, management personnel and others deemed appropriate. It should be done by taking into account all the specific tasks that constitute each transaction and also the relationships between transactions. And it can be made easier by utilizing computer programs.

FLOW-CHARTING

Your first attempt at flow-charting should be to break down the total system into its most normal, natural work processes. This intitial breakdown is very broad and not in great detail. It represents your effort to identify the major overall functions related to achieving the overall mission.

It is important that this first attempt to break down the total system provide the foundation from which future, more detailed, analyses of the system can be made. If the foundation has cracks in it, the entire system will collapse when your analysis reaches the system's finer points. Each successive flow chart must tie together (one overlaying another) in order to ensure that no processes, transactions, segments or elements from the highest level flow charts are left out of subsequent lower levels. You will know you are at the most finite level because there will be no place else to go and nothing else will be needed to be known in order to satisfy the objective or purpose of the system requirements.

So how much should you systematize? Should everything anyone in the organization does have a corresponding written procedure?

A company should have systematized work processes for everything it does that is work-related. This provides universal consistency in its products and services. Before you can educate and train someone how to do something, you first must know what it is you want to do, why you want to do it and how best to do it. Systematizing each work process provides these answers and allows everyone to be trained one right way.

It may be helpful to again cite Matlack. In our flow-charting, we broke the process down to data flows, using data-flow diagrams. We then broke down each process further and further with more detailed data-flow diagrams until each was broken down into its most finite data elements. Each respective data element was then defined in a data dictionary with 22 data element attributes.

The 22 data element attributes are as follows:

Data Element Attributes

1. Data Element Name
2. Data Element Definition
3. Category
4. Alias (AKA) Names
5. Components (of Group Level Elements)
6. Derivation

MIS Attributes

7. Data Store (File) Name
8. Validation
9. Cobol Picture
10. Copybook Name
11. Occurrences
12. Data Store Notes

Operational Attributes

13. Segment
14. Segment Source
15. Actual Source Indicator (Y/N)
16. Where Entered
17. Medium
18. Where Captured
19. Input Documents
20. Entry Screen/Mechanism
21. Output Documents
22. Segment Notes

After compiling the data dictionary, we developed utilization matrices, which are cross-reference reports for each data element attribute that automates the identification of redundancy (useless work) in the Total System Architecture. These utilization matrices become an integral part of the analysis to restructure the necessary useful data elements in the most effective and efficient means possible in order to develop the new Total System Architecture.

Developing a new Total System Architecture can not be done overnight. There must be total commitment to provide for the long-term viability and preservation of the company by making current sacrifices in terms of expending substantial human and monetary resources.

In order for our Total System Architecture restructuring process to be given the thought, time and effort it merited, Matlack put together a new TSA group, which consisted of a quality engineer (or systems engineer) to head up the physical operations side and a Management Information Systems (MIS) professional to head up the MIS side. Other members included MIS system engineer and analyst personnel. This group was, in essence, a research-and-development team charged with the accountability of developing our company's new Total System Architecture and refining it in the future. It had absolutely no accountability whatsoever for any day-to-day operations.

The TSA Project team members took out their flashlights and traced the lines themselves; but they did it together with the input from the field-operations personnel and the MIS operations personnel. All systems were analyzed with the people who did the jobs to ensure that all systems were accounted for; even individual systems that had been developed by individual managers and workers to facilitate the successful execution of their own jobs. As you can see, all company personnel must become involved in developing the new Total System Architecture. TSA totally integrates the systematization of automated MIS operations with the physical field operations.

It took approximately 1 1/2 years for our company to define the existing work processes, but during this time, system improvements were made on a continuous basis as certain segments of the system were revised, assuming revisions were economically feasible at that point of the TSA Project, to comply with the new TSA design.

11. TSA: UNDERSTAND THE FUNCTION AND RELATIONSHIPS OF EVERY POINT OF EVERY SEGMENT OF EVERY TRANS-ACTION

You can understand the function and relationship of every point of every segment by thoroughly documenting the attributes of every system element and its relationship to other elements when you trace the lines. The more attention you pay to your tracing, the more detailed the analysis of the attributes and relationships of each specific system element will be and the better you will understand the function of that system element and its relationship with other elements. This allows you to identify the true need of each system element and to eliminate the unnecessary or useless elements.

As we said before, in analyzing each of these smaller portions, it is important to include and integrate the thinking processes of the human beings who are essential to the proper implementation of "the system"—the universe of the necessary activities needed to achieve the mission. The way the human being naturally performs a work process both mentally and physically must be made an integral part of the system if the system is to be truly understood and is to be ultimately restructured to function as effectively and efficiently as possible. The more complex the system, the more divisions will be necessary. It's easier to analyze a piece of a puzzle when the piece is separated from the rest of the puzzle. But remember, the piece without the puzzle is worthless. The finite points that constitute each segment are integral parts of the body of the system which affect, in varying degrees, the workings of the system and are therefore also affected by total system failure and total system success. Each finite point must be tuned to perfection if the entire system is to operate to perfection.

As an example of how the segment depends upon the system, think of your fingers. The ability to move your fingers (a finite part of your body system) immediately ceases with the loss of life of that body. Similarly, the ability to perform an integral or peripheral function supporting or generated by the total system ceases with total system failure and thrives with total system success.

12. TSA: IDENTIFY USELESS WORK AND ELIMINATE IT

When you are treading to stay afloat in a sea of paper, it's difficult to determine where you're wasting time. Your day is spent plugging holes instead of formulating policy. You're consistently and constantly over-whelmed. But once your system of transactions is pared down to manageable segments and each of the segments is refitted into the newly rebuilt process of Total System Architecture, a vast number of segments will no doubt be superfluous. You'll notice them because they won't fit anywhere. This is the useless work which must be eliminated.

Useless work can also be defined as human or mechanical failure which is preventing the system from operating most effectively and efficiently. It adds unnecessary expense to your operations and costs time and effort that could be diverted to more useful work.

Useless work is identified when you trace the lines of your company's Total System Architecture and analyze each transaction element.

EVERYONE MUST WORK TO ELIMINATE USELESS WORK

Eliminating useless work is a work ethic in which every person in an organization must participate because no one knows the inner workings of a job better than the person who does it. In many cases useless work is created, or improperly eliminated, because management isolates itself. The people doing the work get no say in how their jobs can be improved.

If you improve the job for the employee, then you are making the job more effective, more efficient and more profitable. The job becomes easier and more sensible, and the employee feels appreciated and works harder. If the employee has a problem doing the job, then there is a problem in the system that must be corrected. Therefore, when an employee registers a complaint, you should look at it as an opportunity to improve the system. Employees don't like useless work any more than managers like useless employees.

To succeed in eliminating useless work, management must find out exactly what work is being done, one step at a time, step by step by step, in every transaction, understanding each step's relationships to the others and to the entire system. This is a difficult, laborious, painful task because you have to get into the inner workings of every element of every transaction. Too often we waste our resources improving the secondary or peripheral transactions when the sole purpose of these secondary transactions is to complement the primary transaction and the primary mission. Taking part in the old ''can't see the forest for the trees'' syndrome, many of us lose sight of this complementary relationship and spend all our time refining our brushstrokes as we lose sight of the total picture.

The magnitude of the problem of useless work is apparent. Useless work slows down governments, religions, corporations, schools, labor unions, personal lives, etc. The disease is universal and affects every one of us in our everyday lives. And it's spreading.

SOURCES OF USELESS WORK
The typical causes of useless work are as follows:
1. Demands made on the process that satisfy selfish interests.
2. Incompetent people making changes to the system, attempting to improve it.
3. Duplication of work already in the process.
4. A sudden and/or dramatic change in the process.
5. Improperly trained and educated employees.
6. Ineffective or inefficient system design.

Sources of Useless Work

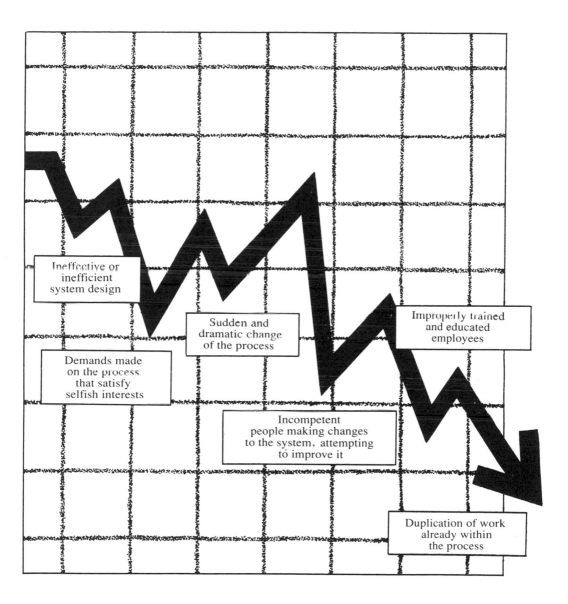

Useless work occurs when demands are made on a system in order to satisfy selfish interests. To appease a large contributor, for example, a new position is created for the contributor's spouse. Immediately, useless work enters the system. The newly created job is not necessary, and the qualifications for a useful job don't necessarily match those of the worker.

Another source of useless work is a change made to a system by incompetent people attempting to improve it. Because these tinkerers don't bother to learn the total concept of the system, but instead are solely interested in making their own mark, the change made often decreases the system's utility and increases its futility. Therefore, when you entrust your employees with the keys to the system you must be sure they are the very best available locksmiths—strong, smart people who will make changes only when changes are warranted. There's an old farmers' adage that says, "You don't tear down the fences until you find out why they were put up."

But useless work also stems from legitimate new requirements made by the system user. These new requirements could come from employees, consumers, management or government agencies. In the process of fulfilling new requirements, however, efforts may be duplicated, thus creating useless work.

Another source is the inherent belief that change must be sudden and complete instead of constant and systematic. This is not true. The cold-turkey method might be good for kicking vices, but it's not necessarily good for improving an organization.

Radical change is not always required for improvement, and there need be no reason to throw away valuable resources for the sake of an overhaul. Frugality and planning are more likely to bring lasting improvement, but systematic change does not require that the change occur at a snail's pace. For the improvement to be worthwhile, it must come through sound system development.

A fifth source of useless work is people who perform tasks without proper training. These people tend not to believe in the system because they don't understand it. Either they were never taught it, were taught it but never learned it, or were taught it but didn't want to learn it. It therefore stands to reason that they will not properly operate within it and will thereby create useless work. Their poor work must then be corrected, and they must be retrained or relocated.

A sixth source of useless work is a system or mechanical failure. But such a breakdown should be no cause for worry. If the system is being controlled properly, a malfunction of mysterious origin should represent an opportunity for improvement. Such a problem forces the system to be examined so that the problem can be determined, isolated and fixed, eliminating future problems and future useless work.

If useless work is not eliminated, the faulty system will be rendered obsolete and will be replaced. On a business level, a company may fail; on a national level, the economy may falter; and on an international level, one philosophy of government may fall prey to another, more effective one.

Once useless work is identified, you have to take the steps necessary to eliminate it. If you deem the function being hampered by useless work is worth retaining, determine the best possible way to perform it. Describe the process. Consider all alternatives and realize that fine tuning of this process is never ending.

In eliminating useless work you will often find resistence. Employees and co-workers will not want to change the way they've been performing work or they will determine that the elimination of the useless work tasks might cause the elimination of their jobs. If you are to gain company-wide compliance there are five things you must do:

1. Communicate the benefits of eliminating useless work via personnel meetings and print correspondence.
2. Educate and train people to perform useful tasks replacing the useless ones.
3. Condition your people before the change and allow time for its acceptance. Change is better accepted if it is gradual rather than abrupt.
4. Compensate your best personnel so that the most talented players on your team sign on.
5. Establish a quality-engineering department and use the quality-engineer positions as a career path to middle level and eventually senior level management.

Once you have motivated everyone to change their wasteful ways and get with the process, you have to keep them with it. Sustaining this effort will be difficult because our society has become so immediate gratification oriented. When your co-workers and employees don't see instantaneous improvement, their enthusiasm and energy will begin to waver. They'll begin to question you and your Total System Architecture.

In order to keep everyone energized and going in the same direction, you must promulgate an attitude that the key to success is continuous ongoing improvement. This mind-set must take over and become a way of life for your organization's personnel. To give your personnel hope, you must use the same methodology company-wide so no one feels as if he is getting all the burdens dumped upon his shoulders. You must also showcase your successes in terms of both people and results. McDonald's sees the importance of putting up a plaque for a kid making minimum wage flipping burgers; so should you. But you should also highlight the individual and the division who made the greatest strides in improving their effectiveness and efficiency—the people who eliminated the most useless work.

So that the task of eliminating useless work does not become too daunting, it is important that you repeatedly stress it can never be achieved to 100 percent perfection. We're human, imperfect by design and nature. **Your objective should be to do more with less; to find better ways to perform the same function.**

AN OUNCE OF PREVENTION II . . .

Useless work is utilizing manpower and equipment resources in reaction to system failures rather than improving the system. *A key to success at any level is the ability to be proactive rather than reactive.* Problems should be anticipated and their potential causes eliminated before they must be corrected. As we refine our systems, we become more innovative, i.e., we find new and better ways to do things. It's useless work to run around putting out fires.

REFINING AND AUTOMATING ARE NOT SYNONYMOUS

It is important to automate a system, but if you automate or computerize a system that is not as effective or efficient as it might be, you may exponentially increase your useless work. Poor system design magnifies all flaws, and as you process more and more transactions faster and faster and faster, ineffective and inefficient systems become that much more dangerous. Little leaks can become tidal waves. Useless work must be stopped in its infant stages. Once the monster is out of control it may be too late.

Automation will allow you to process more data, but if the automation is not properly handled, you will tax your staff with a greater quantity of unnecessary information. Your number crunchers will crack their teeth crunching the wrong numbers.

When designing the architecture of any system, you have to start with the foundation, make sure it is strong, and build upon sound principles.

Then you have to protect those principles as you build. Don't compromise. Don't stray from the course. If you lose your foundation you perpetuate ineffectiveness and inefficiency.

THERE'S THE HUB

Some of the most profitable and successful airlines in the country follow basic principles of eliminating useless work.

If an airline were to fly one half-full plane from Boston to Dallas and another from New York City to Dallas, then it would be running those trips with half-empty planes. Each flight would be operating without a full load of revenue-producing passengers. The same problem might apply to flights from Boston to New Orleans and New York City to New Orleans. Nothing applies during Mardi Gras, or if the Cowboys are in the Super Bowl.

If, however, the airline were to send one plane to Atlanta from Boston and another from New York City, each with full loads of passengers eventually destined for either Dallas or New Orleans, then each of these aircraft is full, and the airline has used one aircraft on each route instead of two. Half the planes, half the pilots, half the crew and half the fuel save the airline half the money.

It might seem that a stopover in Atlanta is creating useless work, since not one of the passengers is headed for Atlanta. But the opposite is true. The airline is looking at the big picture, and the stopover allows the airline to transport its passengers more effectively and efficiently.

USELESS WORK AND THE GOVERNMENT

Useless work is everywhere, but nowhere is it more overwhelming than in our government, which is quickly losing its ability to preserve our fundamental principles of democracy. One reason for this is that our legislators forget they are elected to do a job and instead spend their terms attempting to get re-elected. This is ineffective and inefficient, and so time-consuming that little time is left for legislation. Elected officials, short of time to study the intricacies of their legislation and money to pay for their re-election, too often let their votes be swayed by high-paid and high-paying lobbyists in the palms of special-interest groups. The Silent Majority loses out to the wealthy screaming minority, and government founders.

As you will see later, accountability is essential in any successful organization. A combination of responsibility and trust, accountability is a cornerstone of a democratic society, but it is quickly vanishing from the political climate.

Legislators and voters are losing sight of the fundamentals because of all the demands being made on the system, and nobody is acting as the guardian of the basic principles on which the government was designed. Nobody is held accountable. The bureaucracy reigns. The Army spends $500 on a hammer.

USELESS WORK AND THE JOURNALIST

Newspapers work on a beat system because it is the best way for a reporter to get to know sources and potential stories. How knowledgeable would coverage of Congress be if reporters only drove by the Capitol every 20 minutes. To find out the strengths and weaknesses of a given area, careful, personal attention must be paid. Good reporters, police officers and managers all pride themselves on understanding the way the people they work with tick, on understanding the problems and pressures these people face. It is important to allow them to rub elbows and get to know each other (and their work) and not isolate them at desks piled high with paperwork.

A FEW WORDS ABOUT IBM

IBM is frequently used as an example of a company that does the fundamentals exceedingly well. The architecture of all its internal company systems and product designs is built on a sound foundation. IBM eliminates useless work and systematizes the remaining useful work segments in every internal company system thereby simplifying things, and then automates them.

They don't broadcast that. They don't sell that. What they sell is computerization, not simplification. But without the latter, the former would not be nearly so successful. Just think how many fewer computers and how much less computer capacity IBM would sell if all its customers' systems were simplified before being computerized. But also think how many more customers they would have.

SUCCESS IN SPORTS

In sports, teams that do the fundamentals and eliminate useless work are the winners. Vince Lombardi's philosophy was that you had to do the basic things right, and his Green Bay Packers were known for blocking and tackling better than any other team. Blocking and tackling are the essence of football, and all the fancy alignments don't mean anything if you don't perform this fundamental aspect of the game.

Great players are the ones who focus on and excel at the basics. Pete Rose boiled down hitting a baseball to its purest form, and he did it more effectively than anyone, although others did it more efficiently.

For decades, golfer Gene Littler has been called "the Machine" because of his effortless, mechanical swing. Jimmy Connors, who smashes one ground stroke after another with almost no margin for error, is an example of how far one can go with hard work, concentration and a mastery of the basics. And Tom Seaver has long said that his success and longevity could be attributed to his basic, mechanically sound, pitching delivery. Those who win—in sports, business and life—are those who master the fundamentals.

YOU DESERVE A BREAK TODAY

McDonald's has all the individual segments of food service, from the menu to wall color to cleaning the floors, down to a science. Every move is systematized and spelled out so there is no useless work. Nothing is done that does not work toward providing the customer with the best possible customer-centered quality product and service at the lowest possible cost. And although McDonald's could certainly make a fancier hamburger, they instead make the best possible hamburger at the lowest possible cost to satisfy the demands of the customer. THE CUSTOMER IS ALWAYS RIGHT.

UPS: EFFECTIVENESS AND EFFICIENCY

A company that has nicely systematized the shipping business is UPS. Every single move is engineered, and only the best equipment is used. Important to the elimination of useless work are the proper design, procurement and maintenance of equipment. UPS goes further to eliminate useless work by planning its entire work system—from pickup to delivery —with the overall function in mind. UPS even has, as part of the system, a way the driver should carry the key when he leaves the truck.

We must eliminate useless work in all our work processes in order to remain competitive and survive in the world marketplace.

6

SYSTEMATIZING AND AUTOMATING TOTAL SYSTEM ARCHITECTURE

13. TSA: SYSTEMATIZE

After eliminating the useless work segments, systematize the remaining useful work segments one at a time, step by step by step, restructuring the Total System Architecture and its individual transactions most effectively and efficiently. It is important that your systematization takes into account both effectiveness and efficiency or else you run the risk of automating the wrong steps.

The difference between effectiveness and efficiency is the difference between performing the correct task and performing a task correctly. Put another way, it's the difference between performance with regard to achieving the mission and performance for performance sake.

A truck that travels in a straight line and at the optimal speed limit from Point A to Point B might be 100 percent efficient.

For the truck.

But we are concerned with more than the truck. We're concerned with how the truck performs as a point in our system. We care how the truck runs when it's empty and how it runs when it's full. More importantly, how frequently it does run full.

So this same truck might be 100 percent efficient, but if it's running around empty, it's zero percent effective. If it travels to Point A full but returns to Point B empty, then it is 50 percent effective. And so on.

A baseball pitcher who pitches a perfect game on 27 pitches would be 100 percent effective and 100 percent efficient for he would have accomplished every individual task (an out) on the way to achieving his individual mission (a win) with absolutely no useless work.

Some pitchers give up a lot of hits and walks (inefficient) but win a lot of games (effective) and others throw strikes and get outs (efficient) but don't win (ineffective). As you systematize your operations, you want your people to be both as effective and efficient as they possibly can be.

In order to successfully systematize your useful work elements, you must once again do flow-charting, using the same methodology used when tracing the lines (page 68).

At Matlack, to ensure that their newly designed systems were best, the TSA Project team members were able to check all the best possible alternatives because they knew everything there was to know about the existing system. They also knew everything about the needs of the new system because of the input they had solicited from all areas of the company. And they knew how to get the most out of the new system because of the research they had done to identify the availability of new technology for specific applications.

Comprehensive knowledge of all aspects of the organization is essential to success during reorganization. Check out every alternative system design before deciding which way you wish to proceed. All alternative TSAs must be considered and the best one determined. This process will promote innovation. You don't want your associates to become stagnant and uninterested while you are making profound changes in their work place.

Once a work process has been systematized, the same CCQM methodology is used to maintain and refine it. Remember, however, that the Total System Architecture must allow for the utilization of new technologies that might make a present-day work process superfluous and therefore be able to eliminate work in the future.

Due to the ever-changing world around you, your external and internal environments will change constantly. If your organization is able to adapt and change with them, you will best be able to survive.

THE NEED FOR AUTOMATION

One great thing about the computer is that it doesn't get bored doing the same thing over and over. Innovation is the fun part. Automation is a bore. To free yourself from routine tasks as much as possible and leave yourself more time for the fun stuff, take advantage of the computer whenever possible. Don't just use it. Take advantage of it.

14. TSA: AUTOMATE

Automate the restructured system by computerization (when applicable) or other means.

Although automation allows us to do a greater number of tasks at a faster rate than ever before, it is important to realize that automation is not an automatic answer to improving effectiveness and efficiency. Often automation can cause more problems than it solves because it allows for a greater number of errors in transmission of data and interpretation of data. If you don't understand the mission of your company, a computer will not help you get the point, but—by facilitating the means of collecting useless information—it might help obfuscate it.

Computers are not always perfect for every business, especially small businesses. By carefully examining the needs of your organization, you should be able to determine whether a computer will be right for you. Sometimes, because of economic or technological reasons, a system cannot be completely automated. When possible, these systems can be semiautomated—implementing automation to human decision points, thereby improving the work flow. But don't be scared into an unnecessary purchase by an overzealous salesman who has preached imminent bankruptcy if you don't buy a flotilla of his PCs. Think before you automate. Computers can't think for you.

Assuming you already have a management information system, make sure it is supplementing your operation and not repeating it. Is the computer overburdened with processing duplicate data or data that can be derived from existing data? What about the people doing useless work creating this data?

Automation does more than improve system functions. It becomes an integral part of the system because it locks the methodology in place so that the system must be executed properly, according to design, in order to function. Automation doesn't only increase the speed in which a transaction is processed. It changes how the transaction is processed.

If you are to use the computer effectively and efficiently, you must identify your operation's necessary data elements and how and where they should be captured in the system. Also, where and how do you store them in the computer so they can most effectively and efficiently be retrieved and used as needed to best manage your business?

You can answer these questions only after you have systematized—done an exhaustive TSA analysis of the data elements and their relationships to one another and to the total system. Successful automation requires serious homework.

At Matlack, one of the things we semiautomated was our central-dispatch (operations control) methodology. A computerized system had been used in the past, but it offered the dispatchers a limited view of their operations. Although full automation with computer-generated blowup screens would provide us with a greater field of vision, cost factors have so far precluded us from doing this. Semiautomation, however, allowed us to improve the field of vision and the decision-making process of our dispatchers.

In order to automate correctly, we brought together dispatchers, dispatcher managers, MIS personnel, quality engineering personnel and telecommunications personnel in a fully integrated team effort.

Although it took only a day to initially change over the system, it took approximately six years of learning more and more about our work process to develop and implement the refinements that now exist. We were changing the work culture of the entire company, and such a giant step has to be taken as the understanding and the disciplines of the work processes evolve, one little step at a time. Everyone has to be completely trained. Everyone has to be completely confident. It is absolutely critical that a new system work when it is implemented. Your credibility and the integrity of the system are on the line.

What we actually ended up doing when we automated central dispatch was change over to a card rack system with load and driver cards. These load cards are automatically printed in operations control as new loads are received and entered into the computer system nationwide. Driver cards are automatically computer printed and updated from data entered by the driver into an automated voice-mail system. Dispatchers also send dispatch information to the drivers via the same system.

Now, dispatchers can sense where their equipment, manpower and potential cargo are instantly—as soon as a call comes in. Previously, dispatchers did not have all this information at their fingertips, and would often be unprepared to handle new business or would make the wrong choices in rerouting equipment, causing wasted time and useless work.

With our new dispatch system, we saw resultant improvements in our loaded-mile ratio, wage payments to drivers and ultimately in service to our customers.

◆

For a detailed look at the Total System Architecture methodology see the appendix.

7

MANAGING THE TOTAL SYSTEM ARCHITECTURE

THE NEED FOR ACCOUNTABILITIES

One of the major problems facing every organization large or small is that decisions and decision makers slip through the cracks. The one thing every worker manages to pass is the buck. "It wasn't my idea" has become the credo of the modern bureaucrat, a creature known for his unwillingness to take accountability for anything but a complete success.

Such behavior has to stop. A worker afraid to make mistakes is a worker who's afraid to take chances on possible improvements. He's a player afraid to make the big play. If industry is going to make advances as opposed to clinging for dear life to the status quo, the scale must tip both ways.

Organizations must institute a "no blame, no credit" system whereby workers will have to own up to their failures as well as their successes. Seeing that a gaffe will not result in dismissal or ridicule will foster a better, less neurotic working environment and promote innovation.

Accountability may be hell for the lazy layabout always willing to accept an unwarranted pat on the back, but the honest well-intentioned worker will find the freedom that goes hand in hand with accountability a spur to greater productivity and company loyalty.

15. ESTABLISH INDIVIDUAL ACCOUNTABILITIES

Once you systematize the work process step by step by step down to its most finite elements, you are then, and only then, in position to establish accountabilities for each respective step in the process. The reason for this follows the same logic we've been following throughout the overhaul of your organization: **You must first know what it is you are doing before you can establish who will be accountable to do it.** Until you have the work processes mapped out in their proper order, accountabilities are useless because the wrong people may be held accountable for items which they should have no control over.

In order to determine accountability areas, flow-charting is once again essential because the steps being accounted for and the corresponding accountability areas become clearly visible to everyone. In an organization where there is a properly labeled diagram of organizational accountabilities, it is very difficult to pass the buck because everyone knows exactly what everyone else's role is. **By detailing accountabilities, you add a human element to your schematic because you can now trace not only the lines of the work processes but also the people overseeing the work processes. Every element in the chain now has a human equivalent.** And when something goes wrong, you have not only an event to correct, but a specific person to talk to about the correction. Or worse, a specific person who needs to be retrained or relocated for allowing his area of accountability to falter.

When you determine accountabilities, you should start at the largest accountability area and work your way down the organizational ladder. Just as you want information to flow logically throughout your organization, you want accountabilities to progress reasonably and logically.

CCQM works on both the Trickle-Down and Trickle-Up theories. The organization can be only as good as its top rung because that is where its direction is set. But it can also be only as good as its work force because that is where the direction is followed. Ideas without implementation are nothing more than air. The details have to be sweated from top to bottom.

But unless you're working for and by yourself, you don't have to sweat them all. When each finite detail in your company's work processes is flow-charted, a specific individual is assigned accountability for that finite detail. And everyone within the organization must understand how each individual accountability affects the operation of the entire system and its ability to achieve its overall mission.

This unifying effort helps to sustain the organization: your product and/or service will be improved, your bottom line will be improved, and your work force will be improved.

In assessing accountability areas, you are looking for managers to stand up and be counted for the management of every single step in the work process. You are looking for each and every function to be executed to perfection as the result of specific pre-identified actions executed to perfection by company personnel. Everyone must be able to justify his actions and suffer the consequences—good or bad—for every step of every process of the system. By each person knowing his part and how its execution relates to the success of the whole—by everyone becoming a manager of his functional activity area of accountability—the execution of the function to perfection can become a reality.

It's like turning a typical double play in baseball: the pitcher, shortstop, second baseman and first baseman—each with his own unique functional activity area accountabilities—must be fully aware of the others' roles if the play is to work. Each player must know what he is expected to do under given conditions and how to do it seamlessly in relation to the whole process.

With a runner on first, the pitcher is trying to get the batter to hit a ground ball. If he succeeds in his role and gets that ground ball—say, to the shortstop—the second baseman instantly breaks toward second to receive the shortstop's throw. The shortstop must throw the ball accurately and with the correct velocity so that the second baseman can catch it, avoid the onrushing runner, tag second base, turn and throw to first. On television it looks so easy. But it takes hours of practice and a sound knowledge of the fundamentals.

How often are games lost because the simplest plays are not executed properly? How often are the postgame interviews accompanied by finger-pointing and blame avoidance? The same problems that affect losing sports teams affect losing business teams. And you can avoid many of them by delineating specific functional activity areas and assessing specific account-abilities.

You establish accountability by making sure everyone understands what his job is and how he is going to execute it. You communicate this to your work force by reviewing the flow charts, thereby educating and training each individual with his own accountabilities and those of his co-workers. The training and education should be designed so that each and every trainee becomes involved in training-session discussions and participates in a structured system-wide analysis—learning how he affects the system and how the system affects him. You must make everyone who works within the system and benefits from the system an integral part of the process. In this way he feels accountable for his part of the system and the system as a whole.

The system can be preserved only by the people who work within and benefit from it. And they must be held accountable for its preservation.

THE NEED FOR PERFORMANCE STANDARDS

In order for performance standards to be useful, they must emphasize the success of the mission over the success of the individual parts. Think of a play or movie. A coherent cast with a good script (system) and good direction (leadership) is what makes a hit. How the individual actors read their lines is only a means to an end.

In developing performance standards it is important not simply to stress quantity over quality. Numbers by themselves don't mean anything. What they represent is what's important. Productivity for its own sake is unproductive at best.

16. DEVELOP PERFORMANCE STANDARDS

Once you know the best way to do something and who is accountable to see that the best way is the only way, you can then establish performance standards. Performance standards are the measurement of actual performance compared to standard performance needed to execute a process in a prescribed manner under given conditions.

Because conditions can vary and are not exactly the same each time a process is executed, you need to develop an acceptable range of performance. This is best done by using Statistical Process Control (SPC) charts that identify the upper and lower control limits, within which the process is being executed, according to standard. Outside these parameters the process is not being executed to standard and is "out of control."

Out-of-control processes may be the result of a legitimate abnormal event in the process or of true inefficiency in executing the process as designed.

An example of this would be driving times between two cities such as Philadelphia and New York. The driving time for such a trip—at the same time of day, on the same road—could vary under normal driving conditions. This would set the upper and lower control limits. An accident or a detour would be a legitimate abnormal event. Driving slowly to enjoy the scenery would be an inefficiency.

By identifying and correcting system and human failures, the reasons (root causes) for the plus ($+$) or minus ($-$) deviations in the SPC charts are eliminated, constantly improving the system and bringing the upper and lower control limits closer together, ultimately approaching one—with zero percent deviation, with the system operating as closely to perfection as possible.

At Matlack, we noticed that we had wide deviations in travel time between Philadelphia and New York depending on the time of day. Obviously, you can make the trip quicker at 4 a.m. than at rush hour, but we found that there were times of day during which the trip could be made without much deviation from day to day.

Since scheduling is of utmost importance to a shipper and his customer and it's easier to schedule if you can plan where your trucks are at any given time, we worked with our customers so that they shipped and received loads at times of the day when we had the most consistent, shortest travel times between the cities. This reduced our costs and allowed us to provide more consistent, predictable service. Equally important, it also improved their costs and service.

17. MANAGE THE EXECUTION

When you manage the execution, you manage each step in the work process. You manage in order to ensure that each step is executed to perfection.

Once you have determined the best way to perform a given process, who is accountable to execute each step in that process and developed performance standards to measure how well the process is being executed, you then manage the process to make sure everything functions in accordance with design.

The system is not going to operate on its own. Everything must be managed if the system as a whole is going to be successful. And understanding the purpose and function of each individual transaction and its relationships to the system's many other transactions allows you to manage the right thing.

Now that you've done all this work hiring the best, given them a system to work within that offers them structure but allows them freedom and trained them to implement it, you don't want to start getting careless. The downfall of many a business begins when things—even minor things—are taken for granted. The execution of the system must be managed religiously every single day from now until the end of time. This process is very painful because you must discipline yourself to do all the things your accountabilities require, including—especially—those you don't like to do. But your diligence will pay off with greater effective productivity and efficiency, fewer headaches and more free time.

In order to manage successfully, communication is essential. The operators of the system must understand why it is they do the things they do. If people understand why they are doing something, it is easier to get them to do it.

You must then motivate your people to perform their jobs at the high level you desire on a consistent basis. But in order to motivate, you must get to know your workers on a personal level. You have to understand their respective behavior and value characteristics.

Understanding a worker's behavior shows you how he goes about doing his job and what you—his manager—can do to provide him with the freedom he needs to develop his strengths and the assistance he needs to overcome his weaknesses.

Understanding a worker's values gives you insight into what his internal needs are. In other words, what makes him tick. If learning his behavior teaches you how, learning his values teaches you why. Once you know both, you will be able to formulate individual plans for motivation.

Even once you have everyone sufficiently motivated to work at peak levels, you must constantly coach them, providing them with the guidance they will need to execute their functions and control their activities.

But the benefits will be obvious. When you carefully and correctly manage the execution of a well-defined system, you have the best possible road map to success. You are working in a proactive (planning) environment that, by design, is structured to maximize the utilization of all its resources. You are operating at maximum capacity, performing only useful work elements the most effective and efficient way possible.

There is no better way to perform a given function.

18. AUDIT

You will know when the system fails because part of the CCQM methodology is to audit the system continuously, identifying losses within. If you're constantly on the lookout for breakdowns, you will be ready for them should they occur.

Thus, you will need to audit the system to identify how you are doing compared to plan. If you don't audit, you will not be able to identify system and/or human failures. The system must also be audited to ensure that it is not arbitrarily changed, thereby compromising its integrity. Actual performance must be measured against standards to see how your workers and your organization are stacking up, and a comprehensive audit system must be established to ensure that the useless work that was purged from the system—or new, equally destructive useless work—does not worm its way in. Once you let down your guard, you leave yourself open to the recurrence of problems you worked so hard to eliminate.

In auditing an element or a work process, you must delineate between the performance standards set up for the element or work process and accountability over the element or work process.

1. Accountability is a human analysis. It entails the justifications of actions and the suffering of consequences—good and bad.
2. Performance standards are a result analysis. They can be defined as actual work output compared to standard work output for a given set of conditions, using a given work process.
3. Auditing is a structural analysis. It is the checking process of every single finite element in the work process to ensure it is functioning in accordance with design.

Auditing can be, and often is, drudgery. If the first 17 points are stressed, however, auditing should be quick, painless and ultimately rewarding.

19. IDENTIFY LOSSES

Even with doing all the steps listed, mistakes occasionally happen and losses do occur. Losses must be identified quickly and accurately. All losses, no matter how small, must then be investigated. You can't run your organization like a municipal government, where buses disappear or construction projects go unfinished, and no one notices until an audit is done years later.

Should system or human failure occur, effective and efficient use of the CCQM methodology requires you to take immediate corrective action. After identifying losses you must investigate and treat every incident like a shock loss or catastrophe.

By taking immediate corrective action, the facts regarding the incident are fresh in everyone's mind, providing a better opportunity to trace the loss back to the true loss-initiating event, which was the root cause of the system or human failure. Knowing the root cause allows you to work at preventing a recurrence: you're not just bandaging the wound, you're treating it. Immediate corrective action also allows you to minimize the loss by finding the root cause and getting the system back to full speed as quickly as possible. The sooner you get your operations back to normal, the lower your total losses will be, even if there is an initial one-time high cost associated with immediately bringing your operations back to normal.

Small losses mean that there are breakdowns in the system. A loss for the entire organization means system failure. Treat every unanticipated loss

—large or small—like a major catastrophe and reapply the first 18 points to discover its origins. Do not try to sweep losses under the carpet hoping they'll disappear. Soon the carpet will buckle, and you'll trip and kill yourself.

20. MINIMIZE LOSSES AFTER THEY OCCUR

To do this, you must develop specific system-failure response mechanisms so that you will be prepared for possible losses. There should be detailed plans to follow should a system or human failure occur in order to ensure that system losses are minimized. Failures should be categorized and systematized first from historical data and then from knowledge of other potential areas of possible failures that have not yet occurred. This preplanned, structured response process often becomes part of the system itself to prevent losses from recurring.

The good news is that if you know your organization by this point as well as you should, you will be able to anticipate the most likely spots for losses to occur.

In the same manner that oxygen masks land in your lap when a plane faces problems or Wall Street investors put a stop-loss on a stock purchase, safeguards must be implemented to minimize loss if it occurs. Again, planning ahead is the answer.

21. ASSIGN SPECIFIC LOSSES TO THEIR SPECIFIC AREAS OF ACCOUNTABILITY

Since accountability is essential to the improvement of effective productivity and efficiency we seek, when losses occur, the people accountable must be told of their errors and forced to answer to them and their areas of accountability charged for them. By making the workers own up to their mistakes, they might offer valuable information as to how the losses might have occurred. A fundamental prerequisite to rehabilitation is understanding that what you have done is wrong.

22. EVALUATE PERFORMANCE AND MEASURE AND COMMUNICATE LOSS RESULTS

In communicating loss results, it is important that those accountable for the loss hear the news in a straightforward, businesslike manner and not through the grapevine. One of the major problems facing industry today is failure to communicate, thereby forcing internal worker networks to spring up and prosper. Everybody always seems to know what's going on before anybody officially tells them. This adds secrecy to a worker-manager relationship that should be very up-front and out in the open.

Mistrust of management is an unnecessary hindrance to the work force, and keeping workers, suppliers and users apprised of your results will foster a more cooperative spirit. You're all in this together.

Informing the people you work with about how "their" organization is doing will also let them know how they're doing. If everything is running properly—everyone is working toward accomplishing the mission and not simply filling the hours of the day—the individual evaluations will be rendered superfluous by the announcements of overall results. Again, each person must feel the joy of success and the pain of failure of the entire system.

In addition, specific loss-control objectives can be established based on loss-result analysis which identifies loss-initiating events.

23. CORRECT SYSTEM AND HUMAN FAILURES BY ELIMINAT- ING LOSS-INITIATING EVENTS

Refine. Improve your system. Strive to get better by tracking down and eliminating every single loss-initiating event. Establish loss-control management programs to prevent these losses from recurring.

When you correct system and human failures, it stops them from happening again, and if you eliminate the fear of system and human failure you allow for continual refining, which makes everything better. The upper and lower control limits on your SPC charts will become closer and closer together and ultimately approach one, having zero percent plus or minus deviation, with the system operating as closely to perfection as possible.

◆

So far we have examined problems plaguing many businesses and discussed CCQM, a new and improved way to manage, which will make both your work and your work place more effective and efficient. Next we will look at how you implement CCQM.

PART IV

THE IMPLEMENTATION

8

LAUNCHING CUSTOMER-CENTERED
QUALITY MANAGEMENT

In the early 1980s, Matlack, Inc., was primarily a bulk motor carrier of petroleum products, propane, cement and commodity chemicals. The company was profitable: Matlack had the third highest profit as a total percentage of total revenue within the trucking industry. However, its owners (the Rollins family) were concerned about the company's ability to retain its market share and profitability in a soon-to-be-deregulated industry.

The Rollins family owns many other successful, highly competitive, customer-oriented, financially sound and well-managed companies. They put into place a new management team, of which I was a part, to implement a new approach. The path we took was the basis for what has now become our system of Customer-Centered Quality Management.

THE THREE-PRONGED ATTACK

For starters, we decided on a three-pronged attack involving reorganizing and streamlining management, overhauling business operations and making sales and marketing more responsive to its present and prospective customers.

In conjunction with this restructuring, we established a number of major objectives, focusing on those areas that would have the greatest dollar impact for the company.

- We reorganized and reduced the number of managers, eliminating layers of management that have a tendency to muddle up top-management direction. Layers build up when people are unable to fulfill their accountability and when they want to build up their own little power bases. These additional layers allow managers to put protective nets up so that direction from their superiors never filters down exactly as it is intended. Imagine a large corporate game of "Telephone." Every time the message has to go through another player there is risk of something's being lost, until it reaches the final player having little resemblance to the way it started. By removing

97

layers of management, you make it easier for directions and policies to make their way through your company unimpeded.

- We made the company more responsive from a regional or local standpoint by insisting that regional managers stand on their own two feet and make their own decisions. We also made terminal managers more important and more accountable for their terminal's operations instead of having an army of bureaucrats above them, checking up on them.

- We changed the line of business from a strictly commodity chemical bulk carrier to a specialized carrier of highly service-sensitive materials, hazardous chemicals and hazardous waste, and edible materials requiring purity control. These materials require special handling and high levels of service, so we were forced to revamp our operations with new training, new equipment and a new responsiveness to our customers. The switch to these materials was made because this new and important segment of the trucking industry is higher growth (there's more hazardous, edible purity-controlled and highly service-sensitive material than ever before) and higher profit (specialization, especially when related to these materials, allows for value-added differentiation, which we believe will become more and more important to our customers).

- We improved the operating effectiveness and efficiency of the company by determining the root cause of accidents, developing accident-fault-tree diagrams and implementing loss-control management systems needed to prevent recurrences. This, in turn, allowed us to reduce the frequency of accidents involving our trucks, drivers and cargo, which, in turn, reduced the cost of our insurance liability and increased our company's reliability. By providing a safer environment for our customers *and* our employees, we were able to improve working conditions *and* make ourselves more profitable.

We did this through a number of different steps:

- We improved the hiring process, seeking drivers who met specific behavior requirements. We began looking for people who had steady, deliberate personalities, were precise in their actions and willing to follow orders. The entrepreneurial spirit is to be highly commended, but it is not a desirous trait in a driver hauling hazardous material along a carefully designed route. As part of the improved hiring process, we started drug and alcohol testing all new employees.

- Once we had hired better personnel, we invested heavily in their training. All new employees—drivers, mechanics, management trainees, etc.—were trained, and all old employees were retrained. WE TRAIN EVERYBODY. We began a drivers' training school, which not only touched upon topics related to driving, but also taught drivers how to do their paperwork properly. Forms that are incorrect can slow down an otherwise efficient flow at many points in the system, so it is important that they be done correctly.

Training was essential in our quest to improve loss prevention. Realizing that accidents—vehicular, worker's compensation and cargo—were costing us millions, we designed an accident-fault-tree diagram to identify processes that would prevent accidents and identify what specific steps would be needed to minimize losses should an accident occur.

Two training techniques we used to help prevent accidents were the Matman cartoon character, which demonstrated proper safety procedures in an entertaining way, and the 3-Limb Rule, which states that a worker must always have three limbs in contact with steps or a ladder when climbing. We also began enforcing speed-limit and seat-belt policies. Many motorists correctly live in fear of the 18-wheeler going 80 bearing down on them from behind, so we stressed to our drivers the necessity of safety and routed their trucks so that they wouldn't have to speed to make their appointed times. We emphasized that safety was never to be sacrificed for expediency.

Since a common cause of accidents was workers slipping off the backs of trucks while climbing to hook up their air and electric lines, we worked with Mack Trucks to design a new deck plate to go over the tractors' fuel tanks. We also designed new door grab handles to make it easier and safer for drivers to get in and out of their tractors.

Seat-belt use and speed-limit enforcement coupled with other improved safety techniques helped us eliminate a large number of major accidents. This, in turn, allowed us to lower our insurance rates. Many terminal managers felt that changing insurance rates was impossible. Since Matlack is a self-insured company, to change that mind-set we began to refigure insurance rates on a per terminal basis, offering terminals with better safety records charge-back advantages (the amount the terminals were charged for their insurance) over terminals that were achieving less desirous safety results. Turning individual terminals into profit centers and allowing managers to see their losses change on each monthly statement made them aware that they could make a difference. They therefore took safety more seriously and paid closer attention to the hiring, training and detail work we were trying to emphasize.

We upgraded our equipment by purging our fleet of approximately 1,400 obsolete trailers that were not paying their own way, *completely* refurbishing all the remaining trailers and *completely* rehabilitating our entire fleet of tractors. We also began vacuum testing tank valves before picking up every load to make sure they didn't leak.

The cost of this extensive equipment tune-up was more than $30 million over a three-year period, but it was cheaper than buying a new fleet, and because our fleet was now customized to our needs, it was worth it.

As a result of having better-trained drivers driving better equipment, cargo claims have diminished since 1982, and accidents per million miles have been more than halved.

We upgraded terminal facilities—and we kept them CLEAN—which reduced our environmental liability exposure. We also standardized all new buildings and plumbing systems and beat the Environmental Protection Agency to the punch by removing from the ground all underground tanks.

We upgraded our parking lots. In Matlack parking lots, trucks park on eight inches of solid concrete—which drains into a holding pond—instead of dirt. This way, a leak won't contaminate the ground or an underground water supply.

Contamination through leakage or improper dumping is one of the major problems facing companies that produce and transport hazardous materials and waste. If material in our care contaminates an area and we don't clean it up, the accountability for cleanup goes back to the producer. If a carrier doesn't have the money for cleanup—and the cleanup of hazardous materials can be very costly—the charges again fall on the producer, who almost always has the deeper pockets. It therefore behooves a producer to use a carrier that is less likely to cause an accident and is more likely to clean up after an accident should one occur. Taking responsibility for hazardous materials is not only good for the environment, it's good for business.

This is true of any business, where what's good for all is often good for one. If the person or company who uses your product or service is confident that you will be accountable for all aspects of your product or service —function, safety, etc.—and the close of the transaction will leave said consumer free from worry, you are more likely to make the sale.

We made the decision to address *real* problems by focusing on long-term objectives as opposed to short-term objectives.

These tasks were accomplished by imposing a structured, disciplined environment on one that was previously unstructured.

✦

LAUNCHING CUSTOMER-CENTERED QUALITY MANAGEMENT

In 1982 we began to introduce the CCQM methodology for making the Loss Prevention group more effective and efficient. Some of the steps have been mentioned previously—the fault-tree diagram, terminal training, educating management and publicizing performance—but we have not discussed the response they received.

Upon introducing the first phases of the CCQM methodology, initial reactions of management personnel was very interesting, although not surprising. As we all know, PEOPLE TEND TO RESIST CHANGE. But the keys to implementing a new management system are a belief in that system and the presence of a thick skin. If the methodology works and you are confident enough to sell it, managers will eventually see the light.

The primary complaint heard during the implementation of CCQM was that the methodology was theoretical and not practical. Nothing could be further from the truth. CCQM is completely practical and completely logical. It is not a textbook methodology that has never been tested in the real world. Keep stressing that to yourself and to your team.

In our company, managers and drivers eventually welcomed the structured environment we sought to bring about and the accountability that environment fostered. For example, at first some of our terminal managers thought our new higher standards would make it impossible to hire drivers, but after we went terminal to terminal and had all the individual managers develop behavioral qualifications (ie., integrating them into the process), our mutual interests and needs proved to be the same. And as new and better drivers and managers entered the system free of the old prejudices, those who followed the system got better results. Then the methodology became imbedded in everyone. It took a while, but we never let up.

Progress is often slow, so you should not get discouraged. For weeks and months it will seem like nothing is happening while workers retrain themselves to a new way of thinking, but then WHAM! Think of the process of re-educating your organization as a train climbing a very high mountain. The train expends more and more energy as it climbs higher, but because it is in the clouds, your field of vision is limited and your view is hazy. Then you break through the clouds and you're above all the haze. You have a much wider field of view, and you can see everything more clearly. The world has opened up to you.

IMPLEMENTING CCQM

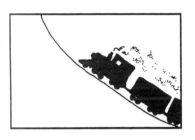

THINK OF THE PROCESS OF RE-EDUCATING
YOUR ORGANIZATION AS A TRAIN CLIMBING
A VERY HIGH MOUNTAIN.

THE TRAIN EXPENDS MORE AND MORE
ENERGY AS IT CLIMBS HIGHER, BUT BECAUSE
IT IS IN THE CLOUDS, YOUR FIELD OF VISION
IS LIMITED AND YOUR VIEW IS HAZY.

THEN YOU BREAK THROUGH THE CLOUDS
AND YOU ARE ABOVE ALL THE HAZE.
YOU HAVE A MUCH WIDER FIELD OF VIEW,
AND YOU CAN SEE EVERYTHING MORE CLEARLY.
THE WORLD HAS OPENED UP TO YOU.

QUALITY

By 1984 quality had become an industry buzz word, with major chemical manufacturers all talking about it, with many different approaches being considered.

We were also talking about quality, customer-centered quality. To get other perspectives, however, senior management personnel attended management seminars with renowned quality consultants like Philip Crosby and W. Edwards Deming. These sessions were helpful not only because they gave us ideas that we could refine for our own use, but also because they offered support for the ideas we were implementing independently.

At a 1984 meeting bringing together a great deal of our staff from across the nation, one of the major topics was what poor quality was actually costing us in terms of performance, business and profits. It became clear to everyone that our financial situation could be improved simply by employing a quality process throughout all functional activity areas of our company. Since the CCQM methodology was proving so successful in cutting insurance losses, company brass agreed to use this methodology for all quality processes of the company.

The benefits of such a move by now should be obvious.

1 - Everyone goes through the same set of steps. Since an objective of CCQM is complete integration of all supplier, producer and user processes, the system works best when there are many interchangeable parts—when people understand not only their own job but how their job fits into the sum of all the jobs.

2 - By using the same methodology throughout the company, a common language develops. One of the frustrating things about overseeing a variety of different departments with different tasks and different missions is that the jargon is different—partly out of necessity, partly out of politics. In the standard bureaucratic structure, with everyone protecting his own back, one of the easiest ways to do that is to make sure no one outside your area ever has a clue how your area does what it does, or better, even knows what it does.

Speaking in code might be effective for spies, but companies function best when internal competition works to improve operations and not obfuscate them.

Many large companies, in an effort to improve operations without going through the tedious work of understanding them, have subscribed to the

"Quality Control" theory, in which a handful of young, well-paid managers are brought in to oversee areas they often know nothing about. It's never made clear to the workers they are overseeing exactly what quality they are there to control, since oftentimes these workers have not even been told there was a problem with the quality as it was. All they know is that there's a new kid in town—an outsider who speaks a manager's language, makes a manager's salary and has a manager's attitude—who's risen to the top of their ladder without ever taking a turn climbing. The workers are resentful, the quality controller is frozen out, and things go back to the way they were except the company has an extra salary on the books.

If everyone in the company is working under the CCQM system, people whose accountability is "Quality Control" are unnecessary because that is everyone's accountability. And since everyone is working together and speaks the same language, a teamwork develops that makes achieving higher quality a reality. From top managers to laborers, everyone becomes a manager of his functional activity area of accountability.

3 - When the same methodology is used company-wide it is easy for people to change their jobs and their departments. This allows you to continually freshen your work force with people you've already come to know and trust. The company gets new ideas and perspectives from workers who understand the mission of the company, and the workers don't stagnate.

4 - Last, and most important, a common approach makes the total integration of all company parts an achievable task.

Specific operations objectives were key parts of the model used for implementing the CCQM methodology. These included minimizing our system's empty miles, maximizing our system's load factor, improving the effective productivity and efficiency of our drivers and improving employee attitudes.

But how did we get the word out?

We developed a CCQM manual, with accompanying video tapes, that flow-charted, explained and gave a structured analysis of each work process, which management used to educate and train all company personnel and identify and correct problems in the system.

We went to every terminal and scheduled training seminars, which got employees excited about the methodology. Regional managers, terminal managers, dispatchers, sales and maintenance personnel, tank cleaners, drivers, etc., were all required to attend these meetings *and* participate. Accountability was established for every step of every work process.

We created a quality engineering group to make certain that the methodology got implemented in all company disciplines.

We implemented a new-hire training process by which every management trainee is forced to trace the lines of the entire system to identify exactly how each and every process works. In the integrated company, you are only as good as your worst manager. Everybody, therefore, has to be at his best.

We used this same methodology, tracing the lines of our system and getting continuous feedback from all those involved in the system to develop a new Total System Architecture, which allowed us to improve our Management Information Systems, determining and eliminating useless work elements that were not necessary to our operation's success.

All these tasks reintroduced the concept of effective and efficient management to our company. Our enthusiasm and hard work got implementation of the methodology rolling, and improved results improved morale, which again improved results, and that kept up the momentum. The next key step was continuing progress without allowing our success to let carelessness slip in.

PERFORMANCE STANDARDS

Once you've got people doing what they are supposed to do, it's important to make sure they continue. Often, workers try harder when a new system is implemented because they know management's eyes are on them. But what happens when the system is no longer new, when the mechanics and tasks have become rote? That's when breakdowns begin to occur.

Customer-Centered Quality Management is not a one-shot wonder. It's not cleaning your room because company is coming, only to let the dust accumulate weeks later. It's not a team that wins a title only to fade away a season later. CCQM is a dynasty. An ingrained philosophy. A way of life. By making the customer the focus of your entire organization, you ensure a continuing relationship with that customer, and your consistency enforces your relationships with your suppliers.

To keep this round-trip circuit permanently integrated, everyone in the chain must know what's expected of him. Always. Performance standards must be developed within the framework of the CCQM methodology: jobs must be clearly defined, accountabilities set and results measured. And these performance standards must be monitored continuously, changing only when the processes themselves or operating conditions change. This constant overseeing and analysis will not only keep you up-to-date on all aspects of your organization but will also provide you with information regarding workers and their success or failure at meeting their set objectives when they come up for performance appraisals.

SUMMARY

To be the best requires a keen focus, a strong belief system, hard work and understanding and following the CCQM methodology.

You have seen the way we began implementation at Matlack, and I hope some of the things we've discussed have forced you to begin to think about what you'll need to do to implement CCQM at your company.

9

COMPANY-WIDE INTEGRATION OF CCQM

THE NEED FOR INTEGRATION

The building of the crescendo to the climax of this methodology of Total System Architecture and our thoughts is the gradual integration of related elements, work processes and universes into a common whole, ultimately functioning as a single universe; as one, utilizing all resources to their maximum capacity to achieve a common mission.

As a system's body of knowledge grows over time from new and additional experiences and research and development, the parameters or limits of its environment change to become part of a larger universe, which the system must adapt to and integrate with in order for the system to continue to most effectively and efficiently function and survive.

Also, as related work processes are typically integrated, initially there is only a small, limited area where there is a commonality in their respective work processes. A continuous better and better understanding by everyone of these related work processes and their relationships as the common body of knowledge continues to grow identifies additional common process elements and allows for their integration, ultimately resulting in a single universe, a single totally integrated process.

By using the Total System Architecture methodology, the beauty of all our efforts begins to blossom and finally comes into full bloom as we evolve from a complicated, disoriented, independent group of processes into a single, totally integrated, coherent, simplified process; as we see the unfolding of the most effective and efficient process and experience its benefits. All elements, work processes and universes become one; part of the same body, feeling the same heartbeat and sharing the same flow of blood.

LET WORK DRIVE YOU

Although you now have various departments within your organization tracing the lines as a first step toward greater effectiveness and efficiency, your job—and the job of Customer-Centered Quality Management—is not

Integration of CCQM

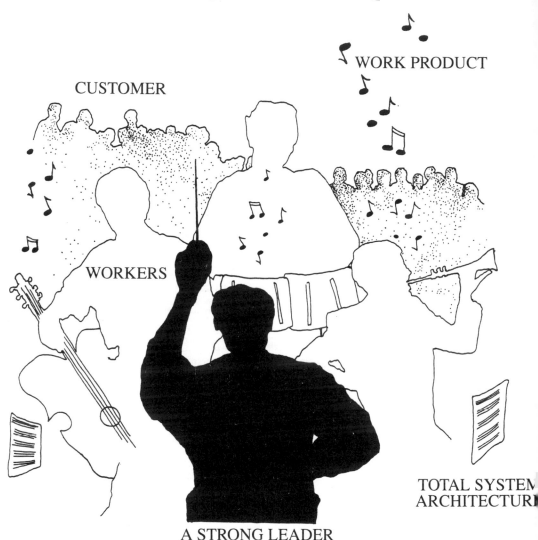

The integration of related elements,
work processes and universes into a common
whole, ultimately functioning as a single universe;
as one, utilizing all resources to their maximum
capacity to achieve a common mission

complete. If you stop here, your company will never function as a coherent whole. Many of your departments will continue to work at cross purposes.

In order to integrate CCQM throughout your company, you must first eliminate the provincialism associated with departmental organization. The way to do this is to make the work process the force that drives your decision-making process.

Establish a company-wide objective and identify the departments affected. Have "Quality" engineers then meet with the specified departments to gain an in-depth understanding of the steps they will go through to perform the required work in the work process. After all the consultations are finished, the engineering team develops an implementation plan and presents it to the group. Once consensus is reached within the group regarding implementation, each department manager signals his commitment by literally signing on to—and dating—the plan. You have established work-process-specific objectives rather than departmentally specific objectives. Organizing work processes at a company-wide level in this manner creates a unity of effort rarely found in large organizations.

By adopting this approach, you will eventually see departmental structure begin to break down and be replaced by enlightened groups of employees organizing around the fulfillment of key company-wide objectives.

THE SEARCH FOR FULFILLMENT or IN IT FOR THE LONG HAUL

At Matlack, minimizing system empty miles became the first company-wide objective targeted for a CCQM approach. After initial studies, we found that long-haul business afforded the best opportunity for success because we already possessed a nationwide network of terminals and cleaning facilities. In addition, there are some inherent profitable plusses to long-haul business:

- The longer the trip, the more time there is to find a return load; therefore, the better the loaded-mile ratio.
- Terminal and pickup costs are a smaller percentage of the revenue derived from the load.
- Cost of cleaning the tankers becomes a smaller percentage of the revenue derived from the load.
- Equipment is utilized on an around-the-clock basis, reducing fixed costs as a percentage of revenue.
- 24-hour utilization also results in lower manpower costs because the effective hourly rates for benefits is reduced.

- Maintenance costs per mile are reduced.
- Drivers are paid based upon miles driven—a built-in productivity standard—as opposed to an hourly rate.
- Management costs are reduced because supervision of terminal-based drivers and tankers is less intensive (they're on the road more and in the terminals less).

EVERYBODY PLAYS

Administration, quality engineering, marketing, sales, finance and control, operations and tank cleaning were some of the departments that were consulted as part of the process of improving our loaded-mile ratio.

Administration provided the resoluteness of purpose and commitment necessary to develop and implement the processes to improve the loaded-mile ratio.

Quality Engineering developed the most effective and efficient work processes required to be executed by all functional activity areas of the company.

Marketing provided the research necessary to identify viable markets from which we could develop the required customer base from which we could procure loads to balance our traffic lanes.

Sales was accountable for getting the customer base to use our service by selling them on the benefits of doing business with us.

Finance and Control provided the necessary accounting required to manage our traffic lanes and measure the improvements of our loaded-mile ratio.

Operations was accountable for planning and executing the pickup and delivery of loads.

Tank Cleaning was charged with making sure all tanks were thoroughly cleaned in a timely manner and available when they were needed for product pickups.

But the key thing was that the driving force to everything we were doing was the work process itself. All accountable functional activity areas of the company were individually executing their department's functions, but instead of achieving objectives specific to their departments, they were achieving objectives specific to the work process of the entire company. This can be done only through integration.

As each department learns more about itself and the other departments and their relationships with each other, its body of knowledge grows. This knowledge allows the separate departments to become more integrated with one another until they eventually become completely integrated and functioning as a single unit.

For example, an accounting work process within the finance and control department may appear to be totally unrelated to and therefore not integrated with an operations department work process which, in fact, is the best source for the data elements utilized in the accounting work process. By the finance and control department and the operations department working together with other departments on work-process-specific objectives, a greater and greater understanding of each other's departments' work processes and their relationships to each other and the whole evolves, integrating the separate departments' work processes into a single common process.

CCQM allows the entire company and each department within it to utilize all its available resources to improve the work process. When this happens, a company is operating on 16 cylinders. This is a company with resoluteness of purpose *and* total commitment. This is the company that will be the low-cost producer in its arena. This is *the* company that will consistently execute most effectively and efficiently.

PROBLEMS, PROBLEMS

Integrating a company around the work process involves enormous organizational change. And as we all know, change can be a painful and problem-plagued process.

Some of the problems that we encountered integrating the various departments' efforts into the work process functions follow.

As part of the integration process, we had to communicate to the company's telemarketers early on what traffic lanes were empty and when so that they could find loads for these empty lanes. We obviously wanted to communicate this information as early as possible so that we'd have more time to solicit customers.

Problem 1 - At the outset, we did not have communications systematized, so we had to develop a system in which our load coordinators (central dispatchers), working out of our central dispatch operations control center, periodically checked for tankers that were not matched with loads. These load coordinators then telefaxed that information to the telemarketers.

Problem 2 - Our central dispatchers were planning their operations only once a day—just before they went home. And whatever they didn't get done

Integration of Intra-Company Departments' Work Processes by Establishing Company-Wide Work-Process-Specific Objectives Rather Than Separate Department-Specific Objectives

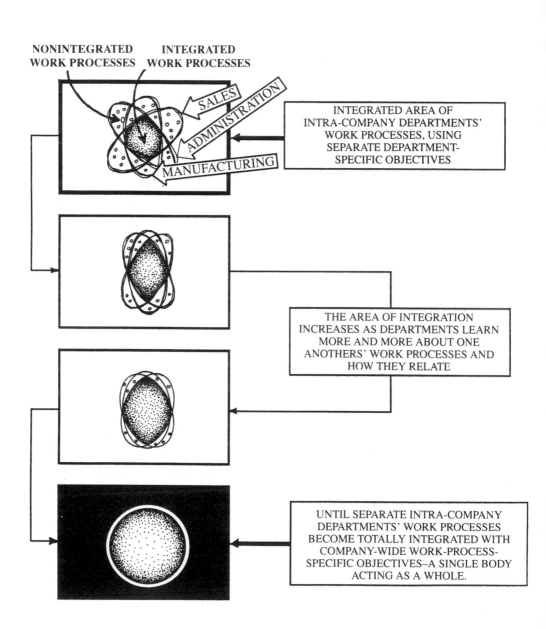

NONINTEGRATED WORK PROCESSES

INTEGRATED WORK PROCESSES

SALES

ADMINISTRATION

MANUFACTURING

INTEGRATED AREA OF INTRA-COMPANY DEPARTMENTS' WORK PROCESSES, USING SEPARATE DEPARTMENT-SPECIFIC OBJECTIVES

THE AREA OF INTEGRATION INCREASES AS DEPARTMENTS LEARN MORE AND MORE ABOUT ONE ANOTHERS' WORK PROCESSES AND HOW THEY RELATE

UNTIL SEPARATE INTRA-COMPANY DEPARTMENTS' WORK PROCESSES BECOME TOTALLY INTEGRATED WITH COMPANY-WIDE WORK-PROCESS-SPECIFIC OBJECTIVES–A SINGLE BODY ACTING AS A WHOLE.

before quitting time remained undone. We corrected this by requiring all dispatchers to plan their operations completely on a continuous basis all day long. Nothing was left to chance. This put our dispatchers into a constant planning mode—like baseball managers thinking a few innings ahead of the present game situation—and this planning ahead allowed us and them to be more proactive in our dispatching and our telemarketing.

WHAT'S THE INCENTIVE?

Initially we implemented an incentive program whereby we compensated central dispatchers and telemarketers only for improvement in our loaded-mile ratio—but in and of itself this went against the total integration CCQM preached—and we soon found that the participants were concentrating so much on loaded-mile ratios that they were paying less attention to our other costs and services. Naturally we didn't want to minimize our system empty miles at the expense of our profits or service, so we changed our incentive program to allow participants to earn additional compensation for improvements in company service and profits in conjunction with loaded-mile ratio.

An incentive program should work toward improving the entire company, not toward improving a department at the expense of the whole.

IDENTIFYING FUNCTIONS—SPECIFICALLY SPEAKING

When the quality engineering department is assigned a project for systematizing a work process such as minimizing system empty miles, the first thing it must do is understand the function that is to be performed and how it relates to the entirety of the company's operations. In Matlack's case, the function is to keep trucks loaded while operating them over the most effective and efficient routes, hauling the most lucrative traffic possible so that the company-owned equipment resources are utilized as fully as possible before subcontracting work.

It is important to identify the function specifically that you want to execute as a result of the work processes you are developing and systematizing because if you do not, you will again find yourself becoming efficient at doing the wrong things. This must be done as part of the Total System Architecture methodology of tracing the lines down to the work processes' most finite elements so that you clearly understand the function of each element.

SYSTEM DEVELOPMENT

Quality engineering is key to the whole CCQM process. It must lead to the assigning of departmental accountability to each step in the work process, which, during the education and training process after system development, must also be assigned to a specific individual. Not only must the engineering department trace the lines; it must also get hands-on experience by going out into the field and learning from the people who do the jobs and must implement the plans.

During the development of our systems, our quality engineering department questioned a cross section of people in our company in order to ensure that everyone's needs were being satisfied. In addition, this company-wide consultation led to agreement that the system methodology created was the best one for achieving our mission. How to do the job was no longer a question.

Once all the work processes were systematized, the quality engineers were able to educate all personnel effectively and efficiently. They were able to train company personnel consistently because they had a written step-by-step-by-step methodology, with accountabilities built in, for all personnel to follow.

When we developed the system, we had maps drawn to illustrate specifically how trucks were to be dispatched from each respective terminal to various areas throughout the country; a specific methodology on how trucks would be dispatched in order to provide the best possible service at the lowest possible cost.

Once the system was developed, we could then develop standards for the system. It is important to understand that these standards are developed after it is determined what is the best way to perform the given functions. You must first find the best way to do something before you set standards and you must let the set standards be determined, using SPC analysis through repetitions of the task performed. We measure our actual performance for doing something against our standard performance, which gives us our efficiency for performing the function the right way.

EXECUTION IS AUTOMATIC

Once we have set standards we can automate the process manually or by computer. This locks in the execution of the work-process methodology so that the work process must be performed according to design in order to operate.

We automated the minimizing of system empty miles by computerizing the load-movement transactions, thereby giving us a clearer understanding of our true traffic-lane imbalances and enabling us to fill these imbalances more effectively and efficiently, substantially increasing our loaded-mile ratio.

When we first implemented the system changes necessary to improve the loaded-mile ratio, we met with resistance at our terminals because each terminal wanted to protect the work it was already doing. No one wanted to give up work or share it with the newly integrated operations of other terminals. This mind-set was eventually overcome when we began convincing terminal personnel of the beneficial results being derived by integrating all terminal operations.

SUPPLIERS, PRODUCERS AND USERS

Having explained the integration of our company's departments into the work processes, we will now explain the integration of our work processes with that of our suppliers and customers (the shippers) and the shippers' customers (the consignees). Just as our internal departments learned more about one another and were therefore better able to serve one another once integration forced them to work together, the same principles apply to the shipper (producer)—transporter (supplier)—customer (user) relationships.

The integration of suppliers, producers and users provides them with the knowledge to further mesh their own resources into the combined work processes and improve all the bonds and the links in the supplier-producer-user chain.

10

INTEGRATING YOUR SUPPLIERS INTO CCQM

PICKING UP THE BOTTOM LINE

To win in a low-margin business it's obvious that you must be effective and efficient at what you do. Sometimes, however, the best efforts of your own personnel are not enough, and the margins you desire remain elusive. At Matlack, one such situation occurred in the area of workers' compensation. We found that we were losing an alarmingly high number of man-days because our truck drivers were slipping and falling off the round fuel tanks on our conventional tractors. Once we identified the problem and determined its root cause, we approached our supplier Mack Trucks with the problem, and with personnel from *both* companies working *together*, we redesigned the deck plate to extend over the fuel tank. Workdays lost because of falling off the trucks all but disappeared, and workers' compensation was brought down to a more reasonable amount.

By working with our supplier to make our environment safer for our employees, we improved our bottom line. Everybody can gain when you work together. In fact, the realization of your objectives is impossible without a close working relationship with your suppliers; so close, if you will, that they become fully integrated into your own work processes where mutual interests overlap.

Another example of our cooperative relationship with Mack came when we discovered that we were having maintenance losses as a result of parts being distributed ineffectively and inefficiently to our terminal shops. By not having parts arrive on a timely basis, trucks were staying out of service longer, and we were often forced to buy parts from local distributors at higher prices in order to get the trucks back in service. Again, by working *with* Mack in our CCQM process, we were able to restructure the er´ parts-procurement and -distribution system in our company an´ resulting in improved service and costs to Matlack. Mack because we no longer had to go anywhere else.

KNOW YOUR SUPPLIERS

We knew we had to formalize our relationships with our suppliers to provide a continuous evaluation and improvement of our integrated work processes if we were to accomplish our company mission "To Provide the Best Possible Customer-Centered Quality Service at the Lowest Possible Cost." We knew this because our company's internal analyses and implementation of improvement were not enough—too often our own improvements were impossible without a corresponding improvement by our suppliers. Also, to improve when our suppliers improved, we had to work together. Our body of knowledge had to be enhanced by those of our suppliers to get the right answers for the best possible solutions.

GETTING STARTED

The first supplier we started our quality partnership with was, of course, Mack Trucks. We began the process by holding a meeting with the presidents and top management personnel from both companies at which both companies took the first step—to make a commitment to allocate the necessary resources to implement the CCQM methodology.

We then were able to go to work. The first thing we decided was who the players would be on the quality project team. Mack had its branch manager, sales manager and product engineer, and Matlack had me, our director of maintenance, director of quality engineering and purchasing manager. We agreed to bring in specific area experts from both of the companies as needs required. It was further agreed that we would have a management team consisting of both Mack and Matlack managers meet every few months to oversee the project team.

The first thing our project team did was agree to a Matlack-Mack team mission: "To Provide the Best Possible Customer-Centered Quality Products and Services at the Lowest Possible Cost." To attain our objectives, we agreed to use the CCQM methodology to integrate the processes of both companies.

Next we developed a flow chart of the necessary ingredients of our relationship, from beginning to end, step by step by step.

The chart began by defining Mack's needs and Matlack's needs in the relationship. In a sense, these were our wedding vows. We then went through the various processes of actually procuring a truck, servicing it and, finally removing it from our fleet. We included safety awareness and evaluation, equipment specifications, equipment acquisition, rehabilitation and/or disposal, an audit operation, product support and, finally, system evaluation before the process repeated itself.

It was important that the needs of both companies be satisfied. We wanted to be sure that each of us was being fairly treated by the other, and we would be better able to do this if we were honest with each other in outlining where each of us was coming from and where we wanted to go.

WHAT'S IN A TRUCK?

Matlack's need was to be provided with the best possible products (i.e., trucks and tractors) and services at the lowest possible cost. To achieve this we agreed that we would have to define the best life cycle of the truck.

- How often would we replace equipment?
- Would we rehabilitate equipment in the cycle before replacement?
- Would new technology make trucks obsolete after a given number of years?

Those are some of the things we needed to evaluate to answer those questions:

- Our scope of operation (How much wear and tear?)
- Statutory requirements (How big? How heavy? How polluting?)
- Maintenance philosophy (How clean? How fixed?)
- Operation environment (How driven? How garaged?)
- Maximization of equipment utilization (How often?)
- Capital restraints (How much?)
- Delivery-date requirements (How soon?)
- Available products and services from Mack (How about someone else?)

WHAT'S IN IT FOR THEM

We determined Mack's needs to be production stability, quantity requirements (economies of scale), delivery requirements, an improved return on investment, single-source supplier, better customer communication (i.e., buying practices, operational requirements [how would the equipment be used?], equipment application [what would it be used for?], purchasing restraints), simplification of chassis specifications, customer component evaluation, component specification justification, knowledge of maintenance procedures and facilities, customer financial position, parts requirements and distribution, training requirements, and new product evaluation/input.

SAFETY FIRST

At Matlack as well as at Mack, safety is the first and most important consideration in all work processes. Therefore, it was not surprising that we agreed to make safety awareness and evaluation the first prerequisite in everything we did together. Safety awareness and evaluation included such things as:

- Regulatory requirements
- Matlack experience, by which we had to identify accident-initiating events and develop loss-control-management systems, including better design of equipment to prevent future losses.
- Mack Trucks' experience, by which they identified accident-initiating events and developed loss-control-management systems in vehicle-recall processes or product-improvement processes.

EQUIPMENT – PROCUREMENT & SERVICING

Equipment specifications was the next item on the flow chart. We all knew that if we wanted the final product to achieve our mission, we had to engineer it accordingly. More precisely, we had to specify exactly what each component part of the truck consisted of to the letter. To do this precisely, we had to consider many factors:

- The operational environment (How would these trucks be driven?)
- The geographical environment (Where would they be driven?)
- The operation requirements (How difficult would they be to run? How expensive?)
- The driver environment (Would they be comfortable over long hauls? Safe?)
- The maintenance philosophy, including serviceability and reparability (Would they break down a lot? Would they be easy to repair?)
- Parts compatibility, availability and supplier support (Would we be able to get what we needed when we needed it?)
- Service engineering, including customer-component evaluation and justification (Basically, would the trucks do what we needed them to do and what our customers needed them to do?)
- Warranty considerations (Who would get stuck paying for a lemon?)
- Delivery requirements (Again, will we get them when we need them?)
- Statutory requirements (Will they be able to travel all the roads and

bridges that they'll need to travel? Will they meet pollution standards? etc.)

We were now ready for equipment acquisition, rehabilitation and/or disposal. In order to do this properly we would again have to examine certain things:

- Current and projected economic conditions (Would we have the money and business to rehabilitate our fleet when we deemed it necessary?)
- Projected marketing strategy (Would we need to?)
- Our current fleet
  - What types of trucks did what?
  - How old was our equipment?
  - Cost of buying new versus rehabilitation?
- Interest and depreciation expense
- Maintenance cost per mile
- Warranty and insurance considerations
- Fuel cost per mile
- Reliability
- Residual value and disposal logistics
- Service support
- Current and projected statutory requirements by geographical location (Would the trucks meet the road restrictions and pollution standards of the future?)

Once we decided our course of action, we had to place the equipment in operation. We needed to determine the accessorial equipment required to be added to the vehicle. Some considerations in this area included the purchase and vendor selection, delivery coordination, installation of accessorial equipment, quality control and final inspection and vehicle-identification decals.

We then got involved in destination logistics such as identifying terminal locations where equipment was to be housed, licensing requirements, delivery notification to terminal facilities (so we didn't have 100 tractors at a terminal that held 30) and notification to Mack Trucks of in-service dates of vehicles (so it didn't deliver 100 tractors when we were expecting 10—or vice versa).

EQUIPMENT-REMOVAL
We now had equipment-disposal considerations, including vehicle trade

package conditions/requirements, notification to Mack Trucks of pickup location and coordination of vehicle trade titles to Mack Trucks. We don't just leave old trucks by the side of the road and let people strip them for parts.

EQUIPMENT-AUDITING

Once we placed the equipment in operation, we had to audit the operation, which included Mack field-engineer support and detailed performance analysis. We also needed product support, which included Mack services, training and distribution of parts, including the associated procedures and paperwork.

We were now ready for our total system evaluation, after which we started the process all over again.

◆

You can see that for Matlack to have done this alone would have been impossible. To get the best results we needed to integrate our processes and needs with those of our suppliers *and* our customers. Total integration is the only way to go.

11

INTEGRATING YOUR CUSTOMERS INTO CCQM

INTEGRATE WITH YOUR CUSTOMERS

In this age of waste (productivity that is ineffective and/or inefficient), using the CCQM methodology to guide the work processes of your own business will definitively differentiate your company from the competition. But to become even more effective and efficient, you need to expand your universe of knowledge to include and integrate with the processes and needs of your customers.

Typically and unfortunately, the only work processes of suppliers, producers and users that are fully integrated are those in which their paperwork intersects and where their transactions take place. All the elements of their work processes, however, are not integrated. The area of integration increases as suppliers, producers and users learn more and more about one anothers' work processes and how they relate until separate company work processes become totally integrated; a single body acting as a whole, a true partnership. Total integration will allow producer, user and supplier to work as one for the benefit of all.

At present it is common for the producer, user and supplier to agree to the producer's and/or user's requirements, and it is the sole accountability of the supplier and/or producer to provide the required product or service. And while allowing the consumer to drive the transaction is in keeping with our capitalist marketplace system, it is not an effective and efficient way for companies that are by choice already dependent upon each other to do business together.

An example of this would be in the shipper (producer)-transporter (supplier)-customer (user) relationship. The shipper, transporter and customer integrate their work processes only where the shipper calls the transporter for a pickup, the transporter picks up the shipment and delivers it to the customer, according to the requirements the shipper and the customer—and separately, the shipper and the transporter—have agreed to.

What's NOT considered is: the total logistics function of procuring the

Integration of Suppliers', Producers' and Users' Work Processes by Establishing Inter-Company Work-Process-Specific Objectives Rather Than Separate Company Work-Process-Specific Objectives

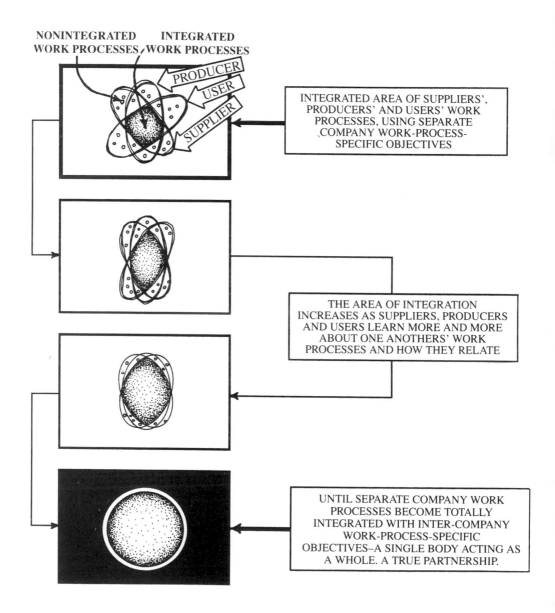

NONINTEGRATED WORK PROCESSES   INTEGRATED WORK PROCESSES

PRODUCER
USER
SUPPLIER

INTEGRATED AREA OF SUPPLIERS', PRODUCERS' AND USERS' WORK PROCESSES, USING SEPARATE COMPANY WORK-PROCESS-SPECIFIC OBJECTIVES

THE AREA OF INTEGRATION INCREASES AS SUPPLIERS, PRODUCERS AND USERS LEARN MORE AND MORE ABOUT ONE ANOTHERS' WORK PROCESSES AND HOW THEY RELATE

UNTIL SEPARATE COMPANY WORK PROCESSES BECOME TOTALLY INTEGRATED WITH INTER-COMPANY WORK-PROCESS-SPECIFIC OBJECTIVES–A SINGLE BODY ACTING AS A WHOLE. A TRUE PARTNERSHIP.

best possible materials at the lowest possible cost for the shipper's production so that the materials arrive safely in the required quantities when needed; providing the customer with safe delivery of the best possible products in the required quantities at the time they are truly needed; and carrying only the absolute minimum inventories necessary to satisfy those needs so that the transporter is not moving excess freight for no purpose. Also not considered are when, where and in what quantities the shipper is going to produce and inventory his products to meet his customers' needs, his own needs and the needs of the transporter.

MAKING THE MOST OF YOUR OPPORTUNITIES

Many times real opportunities to make the respective work processes of the shipper, transporter and customer more effective are lost because all the work processes have not been totally integrated.

Sometimes the shipper's work effort is concentrated on making the work processes more efficient (i.e., making sure the transporter picks up and delivers on time) rather than first making the work processes more effective (i.e., making sure that the transporter picks up and delivers at the *right* time—when the supplier's production and inventories are best prepared for a pickup and the user's needs are best prepared to receive and utilize the goods so that extra time and money are not wasted with goods not yet needed for use). In other words, in these cases the shipper's concerns for efficiency are being concentrated on the wrong thing, and those concerns are driving the transporter to do the wrong thing efficiently.

As an example, a shipper could want to have a quality-oriented partnership but may not want to establish common objectives or integrate his work processes and those of his customers with the transporter. At the same time, the shipper may have wanted to produce a ''zero-defects'' pickup-and-delivery system. Like young married couples who want only the romance and none of the bills, the shipper in this example appears to want all the benefits of a perfect union without putting in the hard work and sharing the information necessary to make that union work.

These situations exist because some shippers are determined to demonstrate to their customers and their internal management that they have a ''quality'' process in place in their company. But this process is merely a facade—going through the motions of a quality process without understanding that they are achieving quality or efficiency in an ineffective work process.

QUESTIONS

What is necessary for the complete integration of Customer-Centered Quality Management in the shipper-transporter-customer chain, is to ask the following questions: Is the shipper or the customer utilizing his storage capacities as effectively as possible? Can storage capacities be changed to make the total integrated work process more effective? Do concentrated delivery times (say, 8 a.m.) put unnecessary burdens on the effective utilization of the shipper's loading facilities and the transporter's effective utilization of his equipment resources? Does the customer really want or need his shipments delivered at 8 a.m.? Can the time window from when the order is taken by the shipper to when the order is delivered to the customer be reduced? How many orders does the shipper lose because customers are aware of this time window but can't work within it? Can the entire work process, including the planning to identify the customers' needs and then satisfy them, be moved up in time to become more proactive rather than reactive, allowing everyone's resources to be more effectively and efficiently utilized?

By answering these questions we make ourselves more competitive and better able to survive. How can companies remain competitive and survive if they don't do these things?

FINDING A PARTNER WHO CARES

At Matlack, one of our customers working *with* us in understanding, implementing and working the CCQM quality process every day is Monsanto, and because of this cooperation, we have been able to achieve a true quality partnership.

Monsanto has established quality teams together with Matlack at different levels throughout our organizations. At the corporate level, the company has worked with Matlack to establish an overall mission and provide the overall management of the CCQM methodology. In addition, Monsanto plant personnel work with Matlack terminal personnel to provide a plant and terminal quality team for each respective plant that does the necessary research required to understand the integrated work processes of both companies and our final customer, and make improvements by changing the existing processes that aren't working. The plant and terminal quality team identifies how the work processes should be improved, then develops the required changes to make the improvements and finally, implements them.

This plant and terminal quality team also meets every month to review the previous month's service failures, identify the root causes of those failures and recommend and implement the changes necessary to correct the system or human failures, preventing these failures from recurring. They also review and correct other identified loss-initiating events.

In addition, as specific assignments are determined by the management quality team, Monsanto and Matlack personnel work with the customer personnel on project quality teams. These teams do the research required to understand the integrated work processes of both companies and the customer and make improvements by changing the existing processes which aren't working. Specialized personnel are brought in to participate as needed. The project quality team identifies how the work processes should be improved, then develops and implements the required changes. Input is received from the management and plant and terminal quality teams as well as from their own efforts. For example, if the plant and terminal quality team is unable to develop and implement necessary changes, it provides a project quality team with information about the problems and possible solutions and allows the project quality team to go to work on finding a way to eliminate the failures.

Monsanto has also invited Matlack personnel to participate on its own internal quality improvement teams.

TRUST IS THE KEY

Matlack established regular monthly meetings between terminal and plant personnel and a corporation-to-corporation quality management team in a structured environment in order to improve service and eliminate the possibility of system failures. Matlack and Monsanto sent representatives to review each other's facilities and operations. Monsanto corporate and plant management even attended and participated in seminars for Matlack management and drivers dealing with training, safety and customer service.

This interaction at all organizational levels opened the lines of communication further so that we learned not only what the other company was doing but what the other was planning to do. This made our working relationship even more proactive. We were always prepared for any changes in Monsanto strategy and/or operations, and they were ready when we considered making a move.

Such a partnership is never easy to establish or maintain. We recognized that we had to feel comfortable with each other and trust each other. We couldn't think that we were taking advantage of each other.

The CCQM structure has allowed each of our respective bodies of knowledge, together with our customers' (the consignees'), to grow and expand, developing a single, totally integrated universe of operations with a common purpose.

In 1990, Matlack was one of a few suppliers worldwide who received Monsanto's prestigious Total Quality Total Partnership Partner Award.

By allowing us to work with them, as Monsanto and many other shippers have done, we are all able to march forward together.

PART V
THE RESULTS

12

PROMISES MADE, RESULTS ATTAINED

In the introduction we stated that this book will teach you how to manage for quality while pursuing the objective of becoming the low-cost producer in your field. Furthermore, we said that once you have implemented CCQM you will:

- Understand your business, its functions and relationships in a way that can only lead to improved decision-making.
- Simplify your work processes so they require less human and system resources to operate.
- Improve your company's profitability because your expenses will be less than those of your competition.
- Force your competition to undergo a major philosophical and organizational change if they hope to compete with you on quality and price.
- Ensure the continued existence of your company as long as the need remains for its primary function.

Let's see how *we* did.

✦

Out of the Top 20 revenue-producing trucking companies in the U.S. in 1980, 13 have gone out of business, three have merged or consolidated, and four have survived and are operating today. That's right, only four out of the Top 20 are operating today.

The primary reason for this is that, in addition to deregulation, there has been overcapacity in the industry for the number of shipments of cargo. This overcapacity has been caused partly by the free entry into the marketplace that deregulation provided and partly by a reduction in the tonnage of cargo being transported.

Matlack has been able to survive in this deregulated environment because we have used the CCQM methodology to improve our effective productivity and efficiency in all company operations. We have not prospered, but we are still here and we have maintained the highest levels of integrity in all our company's operations—refusing to compromise on safety, service or anything else. In fact we have improved our results in all areas, using CCQM.

Matlack has not only been able to survive financially during these tough times, we have also reinvested in improving our company's assets. The effect of these improvements is that Matlack is positioned to prosper in the future when market conditions improve.

SOME EXAMPLES OF IMPROVEMENTS

At Matlack, we eliminated useless work, improving our effective productivity and efficiency a number of ways.

One of the best indicators of success in the bulk trucking business is loaded-mile ratio—the number of loaded miles run divided by the number of total miles run. The more your trucks run empty the more it costs you to accomplish nothing. When operations personnel identified that we were running almost as many non-revenue-producing empty miles as revenue-producing loaded miles, it became clear that improvement was essential.

Following our Total System Architecture—tracing and segmenting the lines—this is what we did:

1. Operations personnel divided a map of the United States into about 80 points through which all traffic flowed.
2. They identified point-to-point traffic lanes where we had consistent non-revenue producing empty movements.
3. They communicated this information to the sales and telemarketing departments to solicit revenue-producing traffic in these unbalanced traffic lanes.
4. Our marketing department priced these empty traffic lanes at appropriate rates in order to attract business to them.
5. Operations also communicated results to sales and telemarketing about specific truck movements. If a truck had dropped off its load and was to return empty we would solicit a revenue-producing return load to balance the lane.

Sounds logical, doesn't it? Eliminate the areas where you are spending money without the opportunity to make money. CCQM showed us the need for a mission and Total System Architecture provided us with a means to accomplish it. It can do the same for you.

All we really did in the five steps just outlined is look at the big picture, trace the lines (in this case our trucking routes), segment them until we were down to finite points (the individual trucks), and then put the system back together eliminating as much of the useless work as possible.

And the results?

In fiscal year 1985, Matlack's loaded-mile ratio was 52.4 percent. In fiscal year 1990, our loaded-mile ratio was 62.3 percent—an improvement of nearly ten percentage points. We run about 120 million miles a year and each empty mile run costs Matlack about one dollar in additional variable expenses. An improvement of one percentage point means a savings of as much as $1.2 million because we are generating revenue on that movement to cover our one dollar per mile additional operating costs that would not be covered if the truck were running empty. This 9.9 percentage point improvement since fiscal year 1985 therefore represents minimum annual savings to Matlack of about $11.9 million.

Such excellent results, however, weren't immediate. As we began implementing the CCQM process at Matlack a few years ago and began improving our loaded-mile ratio, we noticed an odd thing: our bottom line improvement was less than expected. Closer examination told us why.

Even though we had improved our loaded-mile ratio, *our* trucks weren't realizing the greatest benefits. We were too often subcontracting out work and therefore not realizing the desired savings in drivers' wages and other operating expenses. This was useless work. Our equipment was sitting idle while we were paying someone else to haul our goods. In addition, the work we were assigning to subcontractor owner-operators was the most lucrative revenue-producing work in our long haul traffic lanes. Long haul traffic generally offers more opportunity for profit because it increases hours per day utilization of the equipment.

Citing this unexpected problem, we took two steps. No work was subcontracted to owner-operators until all company-owned equipment was first utilized to maximum capacity. And all of the most lucrative work was first assigned to company-owned equipment. The most profitable traffic was assigned to the company-owned units and the less profitable work was subcontracted out—but only after all company-owned equipment was in use. We also began soliciting more long haul business.

The savings?

Our company-owned tractor revenue per unit per day improved from $463 in fiscal year 1986 to $586 in fiscal year 1990, an increase of $123 per unit per day or an improvement of 26.5 percent.

Our company-owned trailer revenue per unit per day improved from

$230 in fiscal year 1986 to $282 in fiscal year 1990. This is an improvement of $52 per unit per day—or 22.6 percent.

Improved utilization of equipment also led to another savings. Since we were paying so much attention to our traffic lanes and the need for balancing loads, and utilizing our company-owned equipment, our terminal non-productive time improved. We reduced delays. Tractors, trailers and drivers didn't sit around waiting for their next assignment. We began paying out less money to our drivers to do nothing. This, coupled with our improved loaded-mile ratio caused our drivers compensation as a percent of revenue to decrease dramatically. In 1985, 37.2 percent of Matlack's revenues went to drivers compensation. By 1990, the number was 32.1 percent. On $220 million in revenue, that 5.1 percentage point improvement saves the company about $11 million a year.

Another savings was safety-related. In a company like ours, accidents are not only useless, they're dangerous. When you're transporting huge tractor-trailers carrying hazardous chemicals millions and millions of miles, accidents may be inevitable, but they have to be avoided at all cost.

When Matlack equipment is involved in an accident, we could lose a valued driver and the use of expensive customized equipment and, should our equipment discharge its cargo, we could also cause possible damage to the environment around the accident. That's why we made accident reduction a top priority. And from 1984 to 1990 we had great success: USDOT accident frequency per million miles decreased nearly two-thirds—from 1.45 to 0.58.

To realize these savings, we developed an accident-fault-tree diagram, which is the structured company methodology for preventing accidents from occurring and minimizing their losses should they occur.

We set out to identify accident initiating events and specific loss control management processes (a speed limit policy, a seat belt policy, etc.) to prevent them from occurring again in the future.

We constantly measured and communicated our accident results to all company personnel via our specially designed Matman comic strip program, shock loss alerts, high frequency accident alerts, training modules on rollovers and other possible equipment mishaps, personal letters to driver's homes from the company president, and more.

We also began hosting safety breakfasts at which we recognized outstanding safety performance with safe driver awards.

In a typical office environment, concern over safety may not be as important as it is in the trucking industry, but keeping your people and your equipment healthy, coming to work and functioning properly will help to eliminate useless down time, and showing real concern for your employees' well-being always pays benefits.

As a last example, we axed useless work by working together with MIS to improve data collection and stop duplicating efforts. We first identified a problem because management reports had statistics that were inconsistent when they were used in different applications. As an example: "total miles driven" on a maintenance report were different from "total miles driven" on a revenue accounting report. The discrepancies were because data was being captured from more than one source and being stored in more than one location.

To correct the problem, system engineers instituted an exhausting 18-month analysis of the integrated MIS and physical operation work processes, seeking places where information was being repeated.

Completion of this analysis allowed us to eliminate useless duplicate work, thereby saving numerous hours of human resources in field and administration operations where time was being wasted and where most monetary savings were realized. Additional savings were made by simplifying and reducing operations internal and external to the computer, which lessened the burden computer operation and maintenance were placing on our work force.

Such computer-generated savings can be found in almost every organization because most companies store data ineffectively and inefficiently —continually duplicating items and filling up computer space, thereby necessitating a capital expense for a bigger computer. Since companies can so easily buy more memory and through-put, they can always have more room for their data. But unless the data being collected is useful data, the increased memory only serves to mask the problem.

Once we have eliminated useless work in a particular work process, we train our people to be better managers with every specific new application of the CCQM methodology. Our people begin to see the benefits derived from using the methodology by the results they obtain, improving their operation. Continual and repetitive use of the methodology soon forces it to become second nature. Then there's no useless time wasted in deliberations —implementation is a reflex. When CCQM becomes second nature, the managers will become true believers, disseminating the CCQM philosophy throughout the company. The CCQM methodology becomes a way of life.

One time-effective and time-efficient method that we've used to communicate positive results in our work processes is voice mail. Since upper-level company personnel are often difficult to reach, we use voice mail to garner results, ask questions and offer pep talks. Voice mail also allows managers to offer a consistent message. When we want something specific to reach our terminal managers, we put it on our voice mail, and they hear it directly from us. We can also monitor the incoming calls to make sure everyone is leaving their results *and* getting our messages. When we receive voice mail communications from each respective manager concerning their operating results and how they achieved them, we select those with the best results and most innovative solutions and distribute the messages throughout the company.

13

CONCEPTS LEARNED

Now that you are familiar with the elements of CCQM, how to manage them and how to integrate them into all your work processes, we would like to detail a variety of miscellaneous concepts to help improve your operations.

◆

ERRORS

What you have read so far is a total process transaction loss-control management system that is effective in minimizing losses in every element of every system, whatever it might be. In every element of a system, no matter how simple or complex, no matter how manual or automated, a large portion of the total work effort is expended in correcting errors made at some point in the system.

CCQM minimizes losses by systematizing all the steps of the process being managed and auditing them so that errors can be identified. In order for these errors to be corrected, they must be identified and investigated thoroughly to determine the origin of the loss-initiating event and the individual or system part that is to be held accountable.

After identification, action must be taken quickly to correct the error where it is causing the problem, rather than where it is effecting a greater failure. This corrective action is a positive action that will prevent the same type of errors from occurring in the future.

◆

EVERYBODY LEARNS

Using our CCQM methodology, everybody learns more about his job, the work process he is part of and the total system. Everyone understands what he is doing as an individual and what the team is doing.

CCQM allows everyone to learn things that will enable him to better understand and execute his job function. He will be able to consider more alternative courses of action that were impossible to consider before because his body of knowledge was limited. No one will be a robot doing meaningless, repetitive work.

The entire CCQM methodology, from tracing the lines to auditing the system, allows everyone to develop a complete understanding of the entire universe of the system and the part he plays in it.

CCQM allows you to streamline your organization. Once the work process is learned by those accountable for its execution, it is unnecessary to have additional layers of management overseeing them. Everyone becomes a manager of his functional activity area of accountability. CCQM allows you to eliminate layers of management.

◆

CREATIVITY

When the drive toward accomplishment in a person's behavior is unleashed with the freedoms provided in Customer-Centered Quality Management and at the same time made compliant by the structure of CCQM, the result of this driving force working against the compliance check causes a creative process. The drive toward accomplishment is forcing the job to be done while the compliance is making sure that everything is being done right, causing a go-no go environment that checks all possible alternatives, finding the best possible one before the process continues.

Creativity is the result of this process of checking all possible alternatives and finding the best possible one. The larger our body of knowledge, the more alternatives we have to choose from, and the greater our degree of creativity.

◆

CAPACITY

As we work the CCQM methodology over and over again, continuously refining the process we are managing, our management system progresses more and more from a reactionary mode after the event to a proactive or planning mode before the event. Following this methodology puts us in the enviable position of having more time to correct fewer system errors.

The more proactive we become and the further ahead in time before the event that we plan, the greater the number of possible alternative solutions that we have to choose from, and the better our opportunity to find and properly execute the best possible way to perform a given function. This creates more space, which is additional capacity in our operations,

DEVELOPING CAPACITY

Utilizing Your Resources
Most Effectively and Efficiently

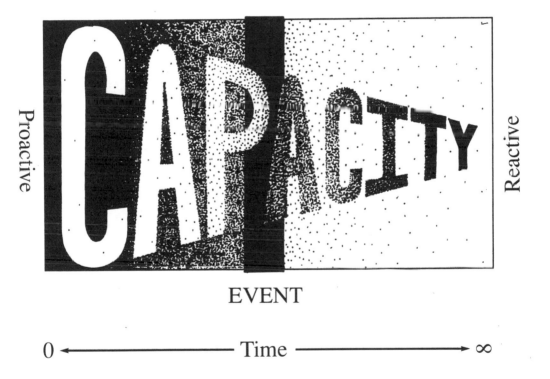

Capacity increases the earlier in time
you plan before the event.

allowing us to maximize the utilization of all our resources, including our human, equipment and facility resources.

By shifting our work into the planning or proactive mode before the event we are managing, we also identify repetitious events in the process and automate them. As we continue working our system, the process becomes progressively more automated and less time-consuming until it finally approaches full or total automation taking zero management time. The pace quickens and there is a greater sense of urgency. As this occurs, we develop greater capacity as managers with more time to manage things of our choice. Also, the process itself develops greater capacity.

Customer-Centered Quality Management gives everybody and everything the capacity to grow. It forces you to stretch beyond your means, constantly making you do more and more.

◆

VISION

CCQM provides you with a broader, more in-depth view of whatever process it is you are examining. This gives you a better understanding of the process, allowing you to see things in a different, better way than your associates.

Your improved vision will give the elements of the process and their relationships a more profound meaning and your ability to decipher and act on these meanings will enable you to rise above the masses.

◆

UNIVERSALITY

The CCQM methodology is a way of life. Its use is timeless, universal and unlimited. Once you begin the process of analyzing, breaking down, re-analyzing, eliminating and rebuilding your work processes, you will see how such thinking extends beyond business applications to the non-business world.

CCQM may be applied everywhere, its uses limited only by our ingenuity. It sets forth simple methods that work. Every time.

◆

DO A DAY'S WORK EVERY DAY

Every day you must process a day's work that your operations generated that day in every step of the work process in every functional activity area of your organization. Every day that you generate a day's work, you must

VISION

CCQM provides you with a broader, more in-depth view of whatever process it is you are examining.

process a day's work. This seems very elementary, but in many organizations it is the root cause for work backing up and being incorrectly processed.

What typically happens is that toward the end of the month or accounting period, there is an increase in the number of transactions executed earlier in the month that must be processed and/or billed. Earlier in the month, these people who are now overloaded sat around with nothing to do. But struck by the end-of-month deluge, errors increase in the rush to get the product or billing out the door and on the books.

This is not effective or efficient. More personnel are required to process these peak loads rather than spreading the work out over the entire period.

In order to get the most effective productivity and efficiency, you must audit the system to ensure that a day's work is being done every day in every functional activity area of your organization.

✦

EXPANSION

The basic concept of what we are trying to achieve doesn't change; what changes with time is the evolution of the system. Innovations, marketplace fluctuations, etc., cause the universe to expand, resulting in the integration of additional universes and their internal processes into the original universe with its original mission. In other words, the system may adapt and the people may adapt, but the mission, assuming it is the proper mission, remains constant. Again, this is why it is so important for the mission to be correct and exact.

New technology is changing faster than ever, providing new vehicles and devices to improve or eliminate operations. CCQM allows you to integrate this new technology into your operations universally, however you choose, without destroying the integrity of the basic principles and architecture of the overall system. Rather than changing your entire system to fit each respective piece of new technology, new technology is the slave to your overall system.

For example, the mission of transportation is to move things from one place to another as quickly and safely as possible and at the lowest cost. Over time, the mode of transportation may change, from horse to car to plane to flying saucer, but the purpose remains the same. The person in need of transportation will then take the information each mode of transport and each alternative (i.e., company) within each mode provides and weigh the

CCQM AFFECTS ALL ORGANIZATIONS

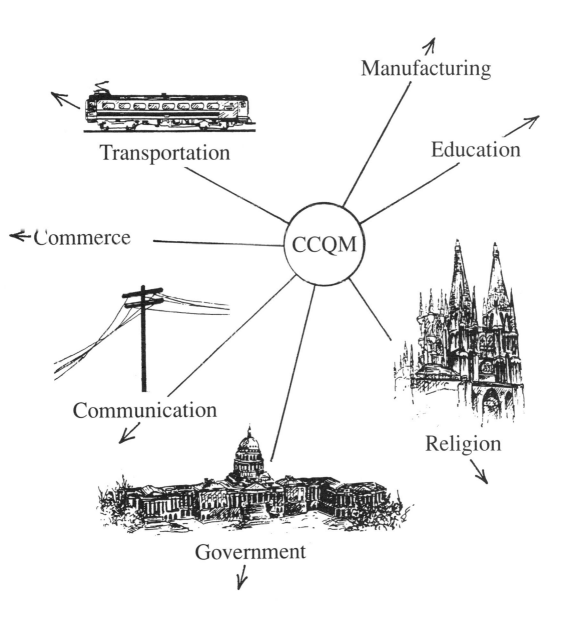

Manufacturing

Transportation

Education

Commerce

CCQM

Communication

Religion

Government

variables—speed, cost, safety—before making a decision. Yes, a plane is often faster than a bus—maybe not anymore—but a bus is often less expensive, and speed is not always the primary need.

The company that provides a product or service at the best price will often have the most business in the short term. But it is the company that provides the best possible customer-centered quality service and products at the lowest possible cost and whose operation is working at full capacity, getting maximum utilization from all its resources in the most lucrative operations before subcontracting work, that will ultimately survive in the long-term, being the low cost producer and most profitable. There are times when subcontracting work is necessary to provide the best possible customer-centered quality service and products at the lowest possible cost; but, if this is the case, you should divest yourself of your unnecessary resources that you have in your organization which provide these functions that are being subcontracted. You can't afford to support the overhead for your unused resources in addition to paying someone else to perform the work that these same resources are capable of performing. In managing your company, it is important to place effectiveness and efficiency as top priorities.

New companies, especially those that are successful, that expand beyond their means system-wise as well as economically, often are out of business before the small struggling outfit that is going three steps back for every one step forward. Expansion just doesn't happen—it too must be approached systematically, with the big picture in mind.

In any universe, everything must grow together or it will destroy itself.

◆

PERCEPTIONS

Customer-Centered Quality Management may appear dictatorial when observed through a telescopic lens because specific individuals are held accountable to a structured system and must bear the burden of accountability for their own specific functions. Because of this structured execution of functions demanded by the system, certain individuals will perceive CCQM as making unfair demands on their time with no opportunity to participate in managerial decision making.

Such a belief is fundamentally incorrect, but when the system of CCQM is first implemented, the constant refining of the process and the sense of urgency to attain desired results force those not willing to fight aggressively for control of their own actions to feel left out in the cold.

But when CCQM is viewed through a wide-angle lens, the democratic aspects come more clearly into focus. Even though functions themselves are being performed in a structured environment, there is total freedom in each functional activity area of accountability to use individual creativity and ingenuity.

As time goes on, this perception becomes the dominant one because the individual gains a better understanding of the total process, overcoming the initial fears inherent in taking command of a function for the first time.

The more the people executing the process of the system of CCQM understand what they're doing and why, the less fear will be a factor in creating negative perceptions.

Also, in your efforts to maintain and improve the integrity of the system, you may be perceived as being insensitive to human needs. In actuality, by preserving the integrity of the system you are providing the best possible working conditions. Human needs will be satisfied with your good work, but your accomplishments will probably receive little recognition. Good news goes unnoticed. Bad news makes the front page. "To thine own self be true."

✦

INSURANCE—or WHAT IF?

An increase in knowledge does not always mean an increase in common sense, but if common sense does not get lost along the way, increased knowledge can often lead to wondrous benefits.

The computer has enabled people to process more information than ever before, but that does not mean a computer is required for every task. Yet when a machine is used correctly, it can facilitate work and provide for greater productivity. When it is used incorrectly, it can cause problems of the magnitude man previously had only in nightmares.

In banking, computer-linked cash machines have made it possible to get money on almost every street corner in the country. Many customers now frequently make use of many bank services without ever seeing a teller or setting foot in a branch office. The purpose of a bank is to store money safely and lend it to people in need. The more people the bank can service, the more successful the bank. Clearly, the convenience of having access to funds everywhere is better than waiting in a long line at lunchtime.

But with every advance comes a problem—spoil the child with gifts and he wants more gifts. Whereas a banker once was a person who knew the family and stamped the passbook, now it's a machine that occasionally says "closed." Now, for the privilege of cashing a check or making a withdrawal anywhere, you must occasionally hear those dreaded words, "I'm sorry, the system is down."

In truth, the system is down only because the machinery is down, and the system, in its effort to please the greatest number of people the greatest amount of time, has weighed the costs and advantages of having backups and alternatives and decided against them. The bank's system is working perfectly, but its equipment occasionally falters.

The system we have outlined in this book never falters, because it is a system that relies not on machinery but on you: your creativity, your diligence, your ability to lead. Yes, from time to time a problem will arise that is beyond your control, but your system should take into account such rare events and provide a method of dealing with them. Airplanes don't look for trouble, but before takeoff you're still warned about your oxygen masks and seat-cushion life preservers. Fireproof high-rises still test the alarms and run fire drills. Just in case. As part of your operation, it is important that you incorporate "be prepared" into your plans and procedures.

Like an uninsured house that gets hit by a tornado, an unprepared business can be wiped out by sudden unexpected misfortune. By doing these three extra system checks you may be able to avoid getting the asbestos concession at the health fair.

1. Continually check your system for safety.
2. Always be on the lookout for new research in your field and constantly do your own research to find a more effective and efficient way to perform the same function.
3. Never take the shortcut approach, because your system is already designed via the most effective and efficient means.

Two sayings about money—"You can pay me now or you can pay me later" and "You get what you pay for"—are very true in the business world. If you find out that something—with your product, in your workplace—is wrong, the amount of money spent to fix it, no matter how great, will be far less the faster you identify the problem and attack it.

If you plan ways to deal with the "acts of God" that can affect your organization, you will more than likely keep those acts from occurring. But you and the people you work with also feel better—and work better—knowing that should disaster strike, you will be ready.

✦

NEGOTIATIONS
When we negotiate a labor contract we arrange preliminary meetings

between the labor and management principals (and negotiating teams) so that each side can see where the other side is coming from. When you understand the needs of the side you are negotiating with, it makes for more effective and efficient negotiations.

Once the stage is set, we identify and break down the negotiations into their most logical, natural contract segments and propose contract language to satisfy the company's needs in resolving these contract issues.

As negotiations progress to address specifics, we identify and document the wants and needs of both management and labor for each open issue. Then we break down the disputed contract sections into their most finite elements where there are differences between management and labor. We identify and document what the differences are, the specific needs of labor, the specific needs of management and how management can satisfy labor's needs in each particular element without compromising the company's position and overall mission. The key is to get to the true root cause of the dispute, the real dispute-initiating event and resolve it fairly, so neither side is compromised. If this can be accomplished, everyone wins.

This is a long, tedious process because both sides need to understand all of the contract sections down to their most finite elements. They also must understand each other's positions regarding disputes and how each finite element of the contract relates to each other and the whole. But, if both sides are honest with each other, the resolution of the problem is obvious and becomes academic. Through understanding we develop mutual trust.

If both sides at the negotiating table understand Customer-Centered Quality Management, it will work. During talks, there are times when labor is the user or customer of management and management must be sensitive to labor's needs. There are times when management is the customer. Management is attempting to sell labor an asset (money, vacation, benefits) and labor is attempting to sell management a service (skill, manpower, etc.). It's important, however, for both sides to be sensitive to the needs of the ultimate customer of the company's products and services.

Insensitivity to these ultimate needs will lead to the deterioration and eventual destruction of the company and the jobs it is providing for all its employees, both labor and management.

These same principles apply when negotiating to buy or sell any product or service. Typical negotiating skills being taught to American business managers stress getting the most for the least from whomever you are negotiating, with total disregard for the needs the parties require to provide for the preservation of the integrity and continuity of the process. Employee incentive plans further encourage efforts to negotiate price reductions to process destructive levels. This thinking is in direct conflict with CCQM.

PART VI

SELLING CCQM
TO YOUR
ORGANIZATION

14

WINNING INTERNAL APPROVAL

Winning Internal Approval for Customer-Centered Quality Management

XYZ Corporation
Income Statements

For Years Ended June 30, 1989 and 1990
(amounts in thousands)

	1989	1990	1990 % Increase
Net sales	$94,313	$102,888	9
Cost of sales	71,516	77,922	9
Gross profit	22,797	24,966	10
Total op. exp.	10,537	12,405	18
Operating profit	12,260	12,561	2
Profit before taxes on income	13,707	14,313	4
Taxes on income	4,500	4,604	2
Net income	$9,207	$9,709	5

XYZ Corporation

XYZ Corporation

A ROSY SITUATION THAT COULD BE ROSIER

Increase Profitability

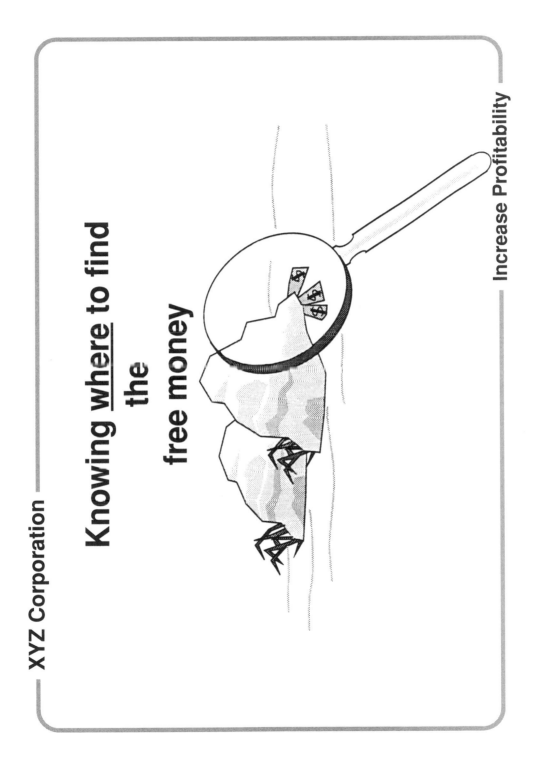

XYZ Corporation

Knowing where to find
the
free money

Increase Profitability

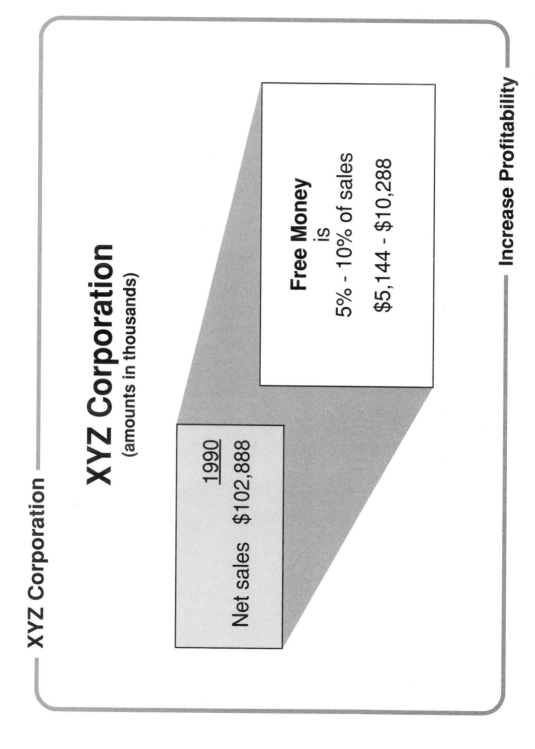

XYZ Corporation

**Acquire free money
by
identifying and controlling
the
cost of quality**

Increase Profitability

XYZ Corporation

Here's <u>how</u> to control cost of quality at XYZ Corporation

Increase Profitability

XYZ Corporation

Cost of quality

- doing work over
- all scrap
- warranty
- complaint handling
- inspection and test
- change notices
  - purchase orders
  - engineering change notices
- etc.

Increase Profitability

XYZ Corporation

Identifying and controlling COQ

leads

to an increase in profits

without:

- increasing sales
- buying new equipment
- hiring additional personnel

Increase Profitability

XYZ Corporation

Here's <u>how</u>

- Establish a winning climate
- Create a focus for the organization
- Introduce a quality process
- Manage the quality process
- Integrate the quality process by involving suppliers and customers

Increase Profitability

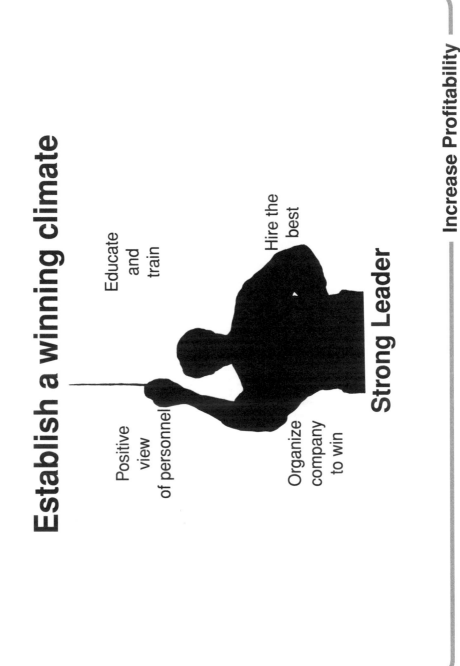

XYZ Corporation

Establish a winning climate

Educate and train

Hire the best

Positive view of personnel

Organize company to win

Strong Leader

Increase Profitability

Establishing a winning climate is really establishing an attitude whereby you

Fix the problem instead of fixing the blame!

XYZ Corporation

Create a focus for the organization

Do the right thing

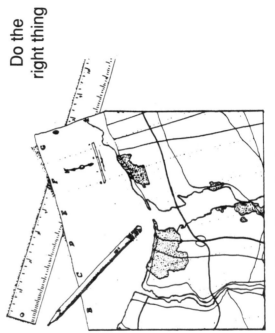

Develop commitment

Establish the mission

Increase Profitability

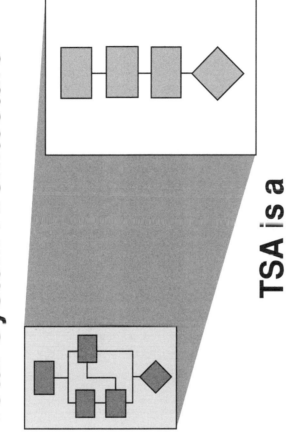

XYZ Corporation

**Introduce
Total System Architecture**

**TSA is a
structured methodology**

Increase Profitability

XYZ Corporation

Increase Profitability

Total System Architecture

- Trace the lines
- Eliminate useless work
- Reorder the parts
- Organize company around the work process

XYZ Corporation

Managing TSA

- Establishing accountabilities
- Developing performance standards
- Managing the execution
- Identifying loss-initiating events
- Correcting all loss-initiating events
- Communicating results

Increase Profitability

MFQAS-7

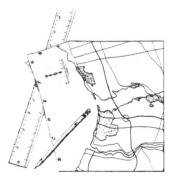

XYZ Corporation

Remember your mission:

**To produce the best
Customer-Centered Quality Management
program at the lowest possible cost**

Increase Profitability

XYZ Corporation

Needed: integration of CCQM process

by

- Implementing CCQM company-wide
- Integrating our key suppliers
- Integrating our customers

Increase Profitability

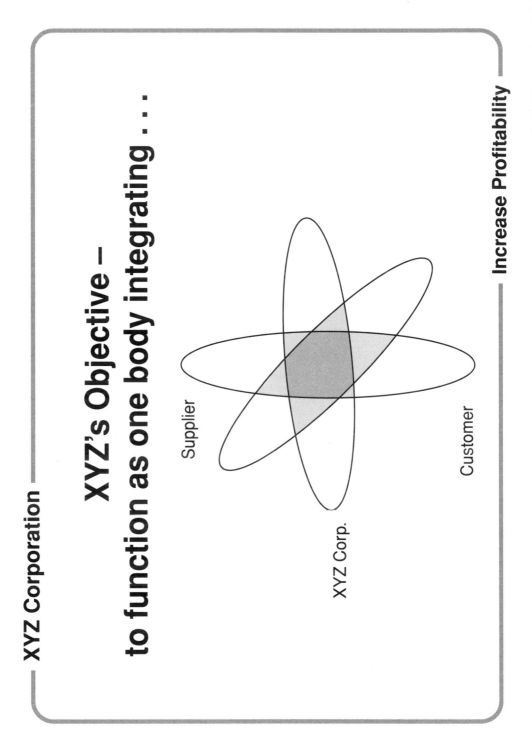

XYZ Corporation

**XYZ's Objective –
to function as one body integrating . . .**

Increase Profitability

Supplier

XYZ Corp.

Customer

XYZ Corporation

In effect, we will learn . . .

- To do more with less
- To find better ways to perform XYZ's functions

Increase Profitability

XYZ Corporation

Results: short-term

- Corporation gains $5,144,000 to $10,288,000 without:

  -increasing sales
  -buying new equipment
  -hiring additional personnel

Increase Profitability

XYZ Corporation

Results: long-term
for XYZ Corporation will be to:

- Improve decision making throughout XYZ because of our detailed knowledge of the business

- Simplify XYZ's work processes so they require less human and system resources to operate

- Improve XYZ's profitability because our expenses will be less than those of our competition

- Force our competition to undergo a major philosophical and organizational change in order to compete with us

- Ensure the continued existence of our organization as long as the need remains for XYZ's primary function

Increase Profitability

XYZ Corporation

Can I have your support and ongoing commitment to CCQM?

Increase Profitability

PART VII

IN SUMMARY

15

FINAL THOUGHTS

The system outlined in this book is democratic because it allows for personal and collective freedoms on all levels.

By adapting CCQM to your own needs, you will make your workers accountable for their actions, able to experiment and innovate and even occasionally err. But you will also create a cohesive work force that functions as a unit with a common purpose in mind.

In our system, every cog, with its complete understanding of the entire process, should be interchangeable. But each individual cog must also be recognized as unique, with the freedom to make its own decisions regarding its segment of the process and also know that its input regarding the entire process will be taken seriously.

The freedom to succeed in a work environment void of politicking is what's needed if we are to get back on track. But the freedom to succeed also allows for the freedom to fail. Failure is one of the necessary evils that accompany freedom. And many times it is only through failure that we come to the greater realizations that propel our advances. Mistakes made while seeking systemic improvements should not be greeted with pink slips or demotions, because without mistakes there will not be many improvements.

This does not mean that mistakes made on a consistent basis or those repeated because of carelessness should be condoned as a normal part of doing business. American government and industry have been making these mistakes for decades, and our failure to correct them has us facing disaster.

Over the next few years the work force is going to have to be given a complete overhaul. The mind-sets and bad habits built up over generations are going to have to be discarded in order to compete effectively. Out will go bureaucrats fattened by life behind a desk, administrators who define their jobs by benefits and sick days, and others—be they union heads, shop stewards or down-and-dirty laborers—who clot the system with three-hour lunches, five-hour coffee breaks and five minutes of productivity. Out will go the pass-the-buck mentality that leads to no results but lots of finger pointing. Out will go the patronage positions. The high-priced kickbacks.

And dysfunctional hierarchies set in granite during the Stone Age.

In place of all this waste will come a totally integrated workplace that stresses the long term over the quick fix, innovation over stagnation, the big picture over the individual ego and the absolute necessity for teamwork.

Above all, the newly totally integrated workplace will stress freedom: to grow and adapt, to goof and to gain—and to allow you to carve out your own little niche of satisfaction and achievement surrounded by, enclosed by and enclosing thousands of others. All that will be counteracting—and enhancing—this freedom is the system set forth to be adapted and implemented by you; a system that tells you first and foremost to understand your mission, or put another way, know why you're doing what you're doing. When you understand your mission, your system will have direction, and all the steps in your process will be purposeful.

It is not an easy task to provide both structure and freedom, but our Founding Fathers managed to hit upon a perfect balance when they wrote our Constitution. American managers are going to have to hit upon the same balance; the different branches of organizations must be given their own accountabilities *and* the power to check and balance other branches *and* a common mission with those branches.

Complete integration of the supplier-producer-user chains is the way we must go if we are to survive as an economic power.

16

EPILOGUE

When I was growing up, I had a friend whose family had a house by the beach. As a frequent visitor to this house, I loved to lie awake at night and listen to the waves as they broke against the shore. True peace—the endless sound of the breaking waves.

As a merchant mariner, I went to sea. And late at night, I would lie atop a smokestack deck and gaze up at the stars. The waves below. The stars above. The gentle rolling of the ship made it seem as if the universe were moving and we were standing still. With the bright stars glowing in the night, it was peace on earth.

At the time I didn't understand the importance of these feelings, but as I grew older, I came to realize that these simple peaceful experiences were encounters with the natural unchanged elements of the universe. The waves had been breaking and stars had been shining since the beginning of history, without any help from mankind. Through wars and plagues and miraculous scientific breakthroughs, these elements have remained unchanged. They have survived the relentless effort of man to improve his environment and, in so doing, to destroy the beauty of its simplicity by contaminating it with impurities.

This book has provided you with step-by-step-by-step instructions to weed out the impurities in your system and start again with your integrity intact and your mission delineated. The task is simple. But it will not be easy. It will, however, be up to you.

APPENDIX

TOTAL SYSTEM
ARCHITECTURE
METHODOLOGY

The Universe of Total System Architecture

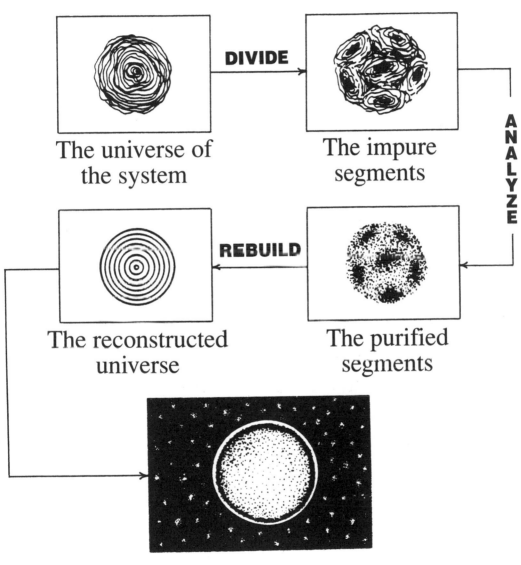

The universe of
the system

DIVIDE

The impure
segments

ANALYZE

The reconstructed
universe

REBUILD

The purified
segments

The Purified Universe

The Elements of Total System Architecture

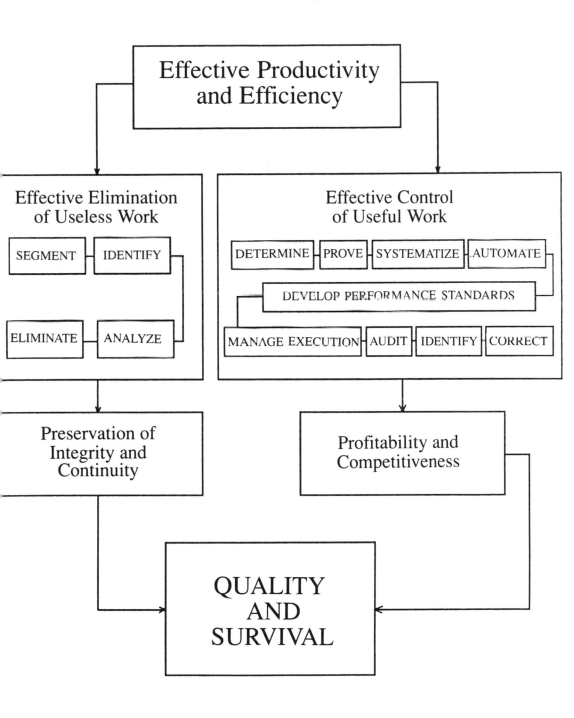

APPENDIX

TOTAL SYSTEM ARCHITECTURE METHODOLOGY

A. Segment the total system.

1. Determine and document the overall mission of the whole system.

B. Break down or divide the whole system into its most logical, natural, smaller work processes (more complex systems can be broken down or divided more than once). A system can consist of a single work process or multiple work processes.

1. Determine and document the function of each work process and how it relates to the other work processes' functions and the overall mission of the whole system.

2. Study every single movement by each work process and between work processes.

3. Document each movement by each work process and between work processes step by step by step.

4. Understand the why, how, when and where of every single movement by each work process, between work processes, and the universe of the system.

C. Break down or divide each work process into its most logical, natural, smaller transactions (more complex work processes can be broken down or divided more than once). A work process can consist of a single transaction or multiple transactions.

1. Determine and document the function of each transaction and how it relates to the other transactions' functions, to the work process functions and the overall mission of the whole system.

2. Study every single movement by each transaction and between transactions, work processes and the universe of the system.

3. Document each movement step by step by step.

4. Understand the why, how, when and where of every single movement.

D. Break down or divide each transaction into its most logical, natural, smaller segments (more complex transactions can be broken down or divided more than once).

1. Determine and document the function of every individual segment and how it relates to the other segments' functions, to the transaction functions, work process functions and to the mission of the whole system.

2. Study every single movement by each segment within and between segments, transactions, work processes and the universe of the system.

3. Document each movement step by step by step.

4. Understand the why, how, when and where of every single movement.

E. Identify every factor that constitutes every segment.

1. Break down or divide each transaction segment into its most logical, natural, smaller finite factors (more complex segments can be broken down or divided more than once).

2. Determine and document the function of each individual segment factor.

3. Determine and document how the individual segment factor's functions relate to each other, the segment functions, the transaction functions, the work process functions and the overall mission of the whole system.

4. Study, understand and document the movement of every single factor within segments. How, why, when and where each occurs and how they affect each other.

5. Understand and document why, how, when and where every single movement of factors in each segment affects every other single movement of factors between AND within each of the other segments, and affects all the system segments, transactions, work processes and the universe of the system.

F. Analyze each respective work process, transaction, segment and segment factor that makes up the system to determine if it is useful work or useless work.

1. Understand and document whether each work process, transaction, segment and segment factor (from here on known simply as the elements) contributes useful work—in and of itself necessary for the system to be

successfully executed—or useless work—work that, if removed, would not affect any necessary pieces.

2. Question how an element can be eliminated and the system still perform its overall mission and function as effectively and efficiently as possible. Elements contributing useless work include duplicate elements and those that can be derived from already existing elements.

3. Understand why, how, when and where elements can be eliminated if they are not necessary for the system to accomplish its overall mission and function in the most effective and efficient way possible.

4. Determine if there are any missing elements that need to be added to the system to allow it to function as effectively and efficiently as possible and add them as necessary.

The purpose of this is to question—and through questioning to understand—the function, relationship and value of work processes, trans-actions or segments of work. By breaking down your workday tasks into tiny pieces and then examining them with a microscope, you are forcing yourself to truly understand your tasks and stop performing the unnecessary ones.

Here also a team concept must come into play. Different people have different perceptions based on their different experiences. Thus, by working through the conflict created by all of these different perceptions we get the best possible resolution.

G. Eliminate any and all elements of the system that perform useless work.

Once useless work is eliminated, the effect on the system will be simplification. Skill is the elimination of the useless.

The results to yourself and your organization of not processing the useless work portions of the system will be reduced costs, increased profits and a better ability to compete. Ultimately, it will result in the preservation of the integrity of the system, allowing it to accomplish its mission the best way possible.

Using the Total System Architecture methodology you force yourself to think and attack your problems instead of reacting to them and allowing them to overwhelm you. You plan or become proactive instead of being reactive. You become a problem solver, and a problem solver can solve any problem. With detailed knowledge of the organization, however, the problem solver can function even better. So learn the details of your organization.

The benefits of being able to execute more transactions faster than ever before will become academic. Capacity will be increased because more will be done in the same amount of time.

The reduced remaining useful work portion of the system will require less powerful, less expensive human and system networks to process the transactions. Smaller, less-sophisticated computers will be required to process the same amount of work. Those saved resources can be applied to doing things of choice.

Now that you have *segmented* the total system, *identified* the elements that constitute the system, *analyzed* every element that constitutes the system and *eliminated* every element that was not performing useful work, it is time to take the remaining elements and utilize them in the way they provide the most production.

The way to maximize effectiveness and efficiency in the system is by taking the useful work elements and positioning them in the best systematic order for the desired process to be accomplished. Inevitably, however, human error will creep in. The system, therefore, must also provide for identifying and correcting the system when human failures occur. Like a chess-playing computer that learns from its mistakes, the system is designed to correct the system.

Maximizing the effectiveness and efficiency of the remaining useful work portion of the system is accomplished as follows:

H. Determine the most accurate, effective and efficient point to capture the useful work elements of the system.

1. Study each element of useful work to determine when, where, why and how it was created in the system.

2. Understand the evolution and function of every useful work element and determine if it is possible to re-create any of the elements in a purer, simpler form.

3. Determine whether each element is captured in its optimal place during the process of the system.

4. Check all alternatives.

Note: The most accurate, effective and efficient point to capture useful work elements is at the point of their creation.

I. Prove the validity of the useful work elements.

1. Break down each useful work element to its roots. Then yank on the roots. See how each element is constructed and if its foundations are solid.

2. Test each element at its roots to make sure its structure and function are valid.

J. Systematize. Create a flow chart for each step of the system's elements from beginning to end.

1. Check all possible alternatives to determine the most effective sequence of steps.

Note: The more creative you are in checking the alternatives, the more likely it is you will correctly determine the best possible sequence. It is important that you approach this task with an open mind, forgetting about the shopworn ideas of the past. Look at the steps before you and be objective about their importance. If they serve no useful function, eliminate them. Then redeploy your excess work capacity in areas that were previously off limits because of a shortage of help.

In checking your alternatives it is important to get input from within the organization. Consultation is a very important psychological component when trying to maximize productivity. It is also important to seek help occasionally from external sources, be they friends, spouses or professionals. A fresh pair of eyes never hurts, and the most inciteful suggestions often come from the most unexpected people.

2. Document the new sequence of steps of the system in a flow chart. The chart will make three things much easier:

a. training

b. accountability

c. auditing

Training will clearly be simpler because everyone will have access to pictures. Everyone will, at a glance, see where he fits in. Everyone will be held accountable for his specific steps in the work processes, knowing how his role in the organization relates to all the other roles. He will see what happens if he misses his work or does his job improperly (note: if the answer is nothing, go back to Step I). He will also know about his job what everyone else knows, thereby eliminating favoritism, double standards and other unfair workplace-related perks, which bring down effective productivity.

Most important, with regard to auditing, this step eliminates the classic

American cop-out, "It's not my job."

It is also important to remember that a chart is just a chart. It is not a brain. It does not make decisions, only conveys decisions in a graphic manner. If, as times change, the chart requires change, change it. Using this methodology will document the necessary constant system improvement. Just because you've put your newly systematized operations down on paper doesn't mean you've retired. Your organizational flow chart is etched in stone only as long as it's maximizing effectiveness and efficiency. Once it has ceased to do this, it is simply another outdated reference source.

K. Automate the restructured system (by computerization or other means).

L. Develop performance standards for executing every element of the system.

1. Measure performance within statistical process control limits for every element of the system for given conditions and develop appropriate SPC charts.

2. Since people can't work at 100 percent capacity all day long, decide, with consultation from your SPC charts, upon reasonable expectations within the upper and lower control limits of your charts.

3. Document them.

4. Explain them.

5. Enforce them.

M. Manage the execution of every element of the system.

Once your system is in place, all elements are equal in importance. For the system to function at premium effectiveness and efficiency, every element must be executed correctly, and you must manage this execution diligently. Proper management here will save you a great deal of time later on.

N. Audit the system on a continuous basis to ensure that the system is being executed properly in accordance with design.

Enforcing performance standards means auditing, and auditing means paying attention. If work is hard, auditing is harder. It's less fun, less glamorous and requires a great deal of both discipline and patience. Auditing also takes tact. One of the most important parts of CCQM is getting the best people to do particular jobs and then allowing them the freedom to make their own advances and mistakes.

So in performing periodic audits, it's important to keep employee morale in mind. And if procedural mistakes are found or performance standards are not being met, make sure that in correcting them you don't throw the baby out with the bath water.

1. To audit effectively and efficiently, use standardized audit checklists derived from the system flow charts.

Notes:

a. Accountabilities must be established to audit the system. If there are no accountabilities, there is nothing to audit except the procedural structure of the system, which, by itself, is worthless.

b. Discipline is required to audit the system. Effective auditing requires a knowledge of the system's overall mission as well as its tiniest elements. Details are important.

c. The most critical accountability in performing the audit is to guard the system against the entry or re-entry of useless work elements.

d. Audit analysis must be comprehensive, and the big picture must always be the guiding force.

O. Through auditing, identify those elements of the system not being executed properly. Identify the true loss-initiating event.

There are four things to look for in identifying what's gone wrong:

1. Identify improper sequences of steps between and within the transaction. If parts arrive when they're not needed or finished products collect dust before delivery or expenses and revenues are on opposite schedules, creating a multitude of cash-flow problems, the sequence of steps in your system is out of order. If each element is operating at full capacity but the elements are out of order, the system as a whole will not be operating at an optimal level.

This is a good time to mention the "just in time" shipping strategy employed by many effective and efficient producers of goods. Just in time means that whatever is needed arrives when it is needed. It doesn't sit around taking up space, and it doesn't show up late to be greeted by an idle work force.

To work on the just in time system, however, requires a system in which all the elements are properly placed. Just in time also requires a fully integrated, fully accountable system that functions consistently from start to finish. Cooperation is also imperative.

But there are many advantages. Warehousing is minimized, product spoilage is decreased, and different parts of an organization acquire hands-on knowledge of how they're all related. In addition, operating just in time forces efficiency because there is tangible evidence when performance standards are not met.

Some of the companies that have made the greatest strides in eliminating useless work operate just in time. It is a good way to go if your system is advanced enough to accept. Just in time is a benefit of proper planning and the effective and efficient utilization of resources. It is not, however, a first step.

2. Identify impurities in particular elements of each transaction. Identifying element impurities comes after you've determined that everything is in order. The key to completing this step successfully is remembering the function of each element so that the ability to achieve the overall mission of the system is not hindered. Impurities can be anything: incorrect data, messages that don't reach their destination on time, wasteful and expensive copies of memos that go unread, travel budgets that go unchecked, etc.

3. Identify system failures between and within the transactions. System failures occur when either of the first two checking procedures doesn't root out the evil. A system failure is much more dangerous than an impure element because the entire system has been affected. Remember, however, that all system failures stem from improper sequences of steps or impure elements. A little piece of the apple rots before the whole.

4. Identify human failures between and within the transactions. If everything so far is fine but things still aren't working the way they're supposed to, chances are human failings are the cause. This systemic problem should be anticipated since the infallible being is a rare commodity, normally found only in mythology. Human failings, however, are often the easiest to correct, because unlike systems or machines, most humans have the ability to reason.

But in many organizations, the reasoning worker is treated like a pariah. Too often management doesn't wish to hear the reasoning of a worker, equating reason with the early phases of revolt. In truth, the reasoning worker should be looked upon as a godsend and showered with affection. Thinking is one of the most important and unique parts of the entire human package.

The key is to direct the thinking in a way that will benefit the organization as opposed to halting its progress. Sometimes the biggest malcontents are not people who only want to cause trouble but people who feel frustrated in their roles, people who have a keen understanding of what they do and what they could do to make both their own productivity and that of the organization better. Identifying human inefficiency—where actual performance does not equal performance standards—often leads to identifying faults in the system, and almost always will lead to a better understanding of the social and psychological problems in the workplace.

P. Correct those elements of the system that have been identified as being executed improperly.

When problems are found, don't use Band-Aid stopgap measures to correct them. Such a short-term means of solving problems will only create greater problems to be solved later. Don't ruin all the hard work you expended cleansing your system of ineffectiveness and inefficiency with a quick-fix solution at the first sign of trouble. Remember, every element of the system is related, and a problem in one element is sure to have an effect somewhere else.

1. Correct improper sequence of steps between and within the transactions. Redesign your flow chart so that steps go in a logical progression and every step forward is not accompanied by half a step back. To do this, carefully examine the points where the system is bogging down and determine whether the problem is due to improper element placement or improper elements. If it's the latter:

2. Correct the impurities of a particular element of the system. Simply re-examine the element and determine if it is required in order to get to the next step. If there is an element clogging the works, cleanse or eliminate it. Keep cleansing and eliminating until the system is in its purest form. Correcting for sequencing and impurities will invariably correct system failures between and within the transactions.

3. Correct human failures between and within the transactions. Correcting human failures requires either a good heart-to-heart talk if the problem is only one worker or a retraining seminar if the problem is widespread. The key components to correcting human failures are often care and patience. Remember, the important word is "human," and humans have brains. If they don't have brains to do what's required of them, that's not their fault, it's yours. You hired them.

When the human failure is a failure to understand an element and its function, the solution is relatively straightforward. Retrain, explaining proper procedures in a different way. Just don't condescend, because then, even if all the employees understand, they still might not produce. Respect is imperative whenever a group of people must work together in order to accomplish something.

When the human failure is merely a by-product of the human condition, solutions become more difficult. Counseling services are sometimes helpful if your organization is big enough to afford them, but sometimes what is needed by the worker is no more than a sense of worth, a sense that his job is important and appreciated and part of a greater effort.

Of course, not everyone can be the star player on a team, but as captain, it is your job to make sure that every player gives 100 percent at all times. But if you free your players of the encumbrances of useless work, explain their new specific roles to them *and* how those roles fit into the entire team effort *and* make them feel part of a winner, your players will respond. Making your organization more effective and efficient takes a team effort, and since the unnecessary team members have been relocated, every remaining team member is equally important to the success of the overall mission of the system.

Total System Architecture Methodology

1.
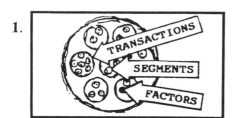

SEGMENT THE TOTAL SYSTEM INTO ITS MOST
LOGICAL, NATURAL, SMALLER TRANSACTIONS,
SEGMENTS AND SEGMENT FACTORS,
IDENTIFYING THEIR RESPECTIVE FUNCTIONS.

2.
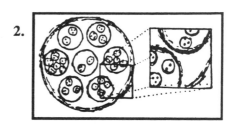

ANALYZE THE SEGMENTED SYSTEM
TO ENSURE USEFULNESS.

3.
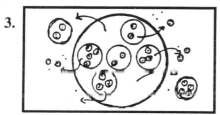

ELIMINATE ANY TRANSACTIONS,
SEGMENTS AND SEGMENT FACTORS
THAT PERFORM USELESS WORK.

4.
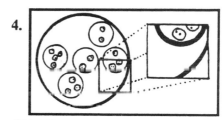

ANALYZE THE REMAINING TRANSACTIONS,
SEGMENTS AND SEGMENT FACTORS TO
DETERMINE WHERE TO CAPTURE THEM IN
THE SYSTEM AND TO PROVE THEIR VALIDITY.

5.
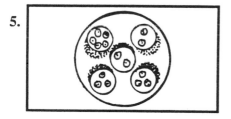

SYSTEMATIZE THE SYSTEM'S
REMAINING TRANSACTIONS, SEGMENTS
AND SEGMENT FACTORS.

6.
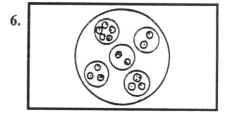

AUTOMATE THE SYSTEM.

7.
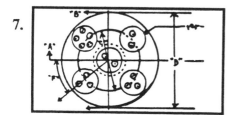

DEVELOP PERFORMANCE STANDARDS AND
MANAGE THE EXECUTION OF EVERY
TRANSACTION, SEGMENT AND SEGMENT FACTOR.

8.
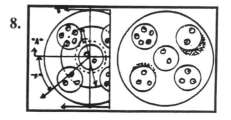

AUDIT THE SYSTEM.